LIVING THE FRUIT OF THE SPIRIT

How God's Grace Can Transform Your World

Joshua M. Danis

the WORD among us®
press

Published by The Word Among Us Press
7115 Guilford Drive, Suite 100
Frederick, Maryland 21704
wau.org

24 23 22 21 20   1 2 3 4 5

ISBN: 978-1-59325-499-5
eISBN: 978-1-59325-512-1

Cover design by Suzanne Earl
Text design by David Crosson

Made and printed in the United States of America

Library of Congress Control Number: 2020911260

DEDICATION

I want to dedicate this book to my father-in-law, Harold, and my father, Mark. Though so different from each other, both have fathered me by the model of fruit being born in their own lives.

CONTENTS

CHAPTER 1

Transformed by Grace

Looking back, I find it incredible that my parents gave me such a generous high school graduation gift: a two-week pilgrimage through Europe with my father. My most memorable moment of the trip, however, was unplanned. Realizing we had a full three-hour layover at the airport in Amsterdam, we seized the opportunity to take a taxi to a beautiful old church in the Catholic Diocese of Haarlem-Amsterdam. Our plan was to go straight there and then grab some lunch.

Sadly, when we arrived, we found that the doors of the church were not only locked but actually barred shut. A passerby told us that this priceless piece of heritage could no longer afford to stay open year-round. We had traveled to Europe specifically to visit the holy places where God had done great work in the past. Here we saw that faith communities can also find themselves on the verge of dying. It pierced my heart.

Be of Good Hope

I don't mean to discourage you. I actually want to begin this book with a spark of hope . . . and also a bit of a confession. You see, I used to believe that the Church today is incapable of renewal. I accepted the fact that we lived in a time of declining Church membership, and I felt that there was nothing we could do about it. Perhaps, in a few hundred years, the Church might be in a better position to make a positive difference in the world. I repent of such a cynical notion. I apologize for the ways that I let this hopeless attitude impact my decisions as a worker in the kingdom.

I now accept that God can move in any time and season, however he sees fit. The story of this generation's participation in the history of the Church cannot be told before it has even happened! No one can say, in advance, that we slept through our pivotal stage of human history. God is moving now in the lives of Christians and nonbelievers alike. I have witnessed parish communities becoming revitalized and recapturing their missionary call. I now believe that we might be living in a season of great opportunity, perhaps even the greatest season of opportunity the Church has ever known.

I know there are many who may still feel the way I used to feel. They see a culture of secularism that rejects not only Christianity but also the very idea of God. They see laws and social practices that run counter to the gospel, and they conclude that the world is doomed. Some have argued that it's the responsibility of the Church to hunker down and wait it out until things get better. They point to the fact that fewer and fewer young people attend church or consider themselves believers, or they talk about the moral failures of some leaders. In light of a toxic culture and weakened society, these Christians argue that we should bury the treasure of faith in our churches until a sunnier time.

Because I once held a similar position, I feel particularly responsible to speak up. We have a God-given commission to "Go, . . . and make disciples of all nations" (Matthew 28:19). Yet many today wonder if this is really the right time for the Church to renew its efforts. Shouldn't we work on our public relations first? I say now is the perfect time because it is the present, and the present is the only time we will ever have available to us. There are souls out there who are hurting, struggling, aching, and longing for the joy that can only come from the gospel. They may not be able to wait until our approval ratings go up. We have the sacred duty to reach out to them today, regardless of any reluctance we might feel.

An Honest Look at the Challenge

Nevertheless, we shouldn't look at the challenges before us with idealistic naiveté. Recently, I spoke with a young priest friend who had just been named a pastor. One of the first things he did was look back through twenty-five years of records for his parish. He was shocked to discover that despite his parish being considered one of the strongest in his diocese, the records showed a consistent year-over-year decline in every significant measure available—church attendance, baptisms, confirmations, weddings, and even funerals. With a look of determination, he told me that unless we are willing to change, the current rate of decline would mean that his parish would disappear by 2040.

Today I work for Alpha, an organization dedicated to introducing people, through hospitality and open conversation, to the good news of Jesus' life, death, and resurrection. In my travels for Alpha, I have met many people who share stories of loved ones far from God. They tell me, sometimes with tears in their eyes, about their longing to see their children or spouses come to the fullness of a relationship with Christ. They rightly bemoan the abuse crisis that has devastated victims, their families, and the Church. Yet God is still God. It is only in the encounter of deep, intimate connection with him that we will find fulfillment in this life and the next.

Many of these passionate people have become students of evangelization. They study Church teaching and come to a deep understanding of doctrine. They even practice what to say and what not to say to those who are far from Christ. The Church, for its part, has likewise responded with an impressive vigor and intentionality. Offices of evangelization have cropped up all over the country. Books and programs support these initiatives, and some institutions even offer degrees or certificates in evangelization.

The Three Es of Unfinished Evangelization

This new thrust in favor of evangelizing has its downside however. Just as you can find get-rich-quick schemes anywhere, so also you can find apparent shortcuts to fulfilling the Church's call to evangelization. There are three such shortcuts that can oversimplify the process: events, experts, and explanations. Each has a role to play, but in and of themselves, they are grossly insufficient to the task of sharing Christ.

Events

Churches love to host events. We use music, lighting, and a clever or impassioned message to get people's attention. Sometimes we hold out a carrot, such as Confirmation or marriage preparation, for which they must run a gauntlet of our events. Then we hope that what they learn there will forever change their lives. And you know what? Sometimes it works! A few of the people who attend our mandatory or heavily promoted events and retreats hear something that makes them think. They then follow up with us and begin a relationship that leads them to encounter Jesus in a powerful and life-changing way.

But too often, we spend most of our time and energy on events despite their diminishing returns. We try harder, hosting more or larger events, not really understanding our audience. Some who attend carry heavy grudges or burdens that make them ill prepared to receive what we offer. Others may receive a positive message, but too often it's a one-time encounter, a momentary flash of clarity in the chaos of a hectic and demanding life. There's no post-event continuity to support their ongoing search and struggle.

I used to work for the Archdiocese of Cincinnati. On one occasion, the staff reviewed some of the compelling statistical information that showed how our event-based faith formation methods were no longer working. We all felt convinced about the need to change our approach and immediately started to brainstorm the options. A few moments later, we had a good laugh at ourselves. Would you like to guess the very first solution we proposed? Hosting another event! Events can be part of the solution when used well, but they are not the solution. Events are nothing more than a tool, and an introductory tool at that.

My wife, Hollie, is a youth minister, and she said it best, as she so often does. She feels that all the time, energy, effort, and resources she and her team put into hosting big events have simply been a means to create a few moments of honest, unstructured relationship building. She has since begun to shift away from event-focused youth ministry in order to embrace what she calls relationship-focused youth ministry.

Experts

Recently, I spent some time with Fr. Michael Schmitz, chaplain for the Newman Center at the University of Minnesota, Duluth, and a popular speaker and evangelist. I would be hard-pressed to find a better expert than Fr. Mike. He is articulate. He is gracious. He is funny and even humble. Best of all, you can tell when you're with him that he cares deeply about people, longing to honor them and connect them to Jesus.

Yet even he sees a trend regarding "experts" that concerns him. He says many of the young people at his college campus want to introduce their non-Christian friends to *him*. They hope that if their friends visit with Fr. Mike for awhile, his presence and words will win them over to Jesus. Now, of course Fr. Mike works hard to make himself available and wants to do everything he can to facilitate conversion, but he knows it cannot revolve around him.

Further, Fr. Mike, as with any expert or evangelist, faces a significant scalability problem. If nothing else, we are all limited by time and space—we can't be everywhere at once. Experts like Fr. Mike are awesome, but how much richer the outreach if we all became like Fr. Mike to the people we encounter!

We tend to rely far too often on experts. We give out books and videos, and we recommend podcasts and other media because we think that the experts will win people over more readily than the witness of our own lives. A director of religious education once told me, tearfully, that she felt she had been doing her work all wrong for decades. "Basically, I've been telling parents that I am the expert," she said. "If they bring their kids to church once a week, I will make them good Christians."

Now, don't get me wrong; we have some amazing experts who are doing a wonderful job modeling and teaching the faith, but the work is too grand for us to rely solely on them. We need so much more than just experts. We need each of us.

Explanations

When I was in high school, I spent about two years devouring apologetics and basic theology. I studied all the right Bible verses and analogies so that I'd be ready for any question. I was sure I knew the proper logical arguments to answer atheists, Jews, Muslims, and even other Christians. Every time I gained some new insight, I felt this little rush of excitement. What a wondrously complex and beautiful God we serve! To this day, I am grateful for that season of discovery during which I was able to unpack many of the mysteries of our all-powerful God.

And yet deep down, even then I knew I was giving unreasonable priority to my study. I was spending far more time learning about Jesus than being with Jesus. I also began to notice that most people didn't care too much for my answers. Sometimes they just found them less convincing than I did. Other times they would even say I was right but that they didn't care. In fact, I would have to admit that my occasionally uncharitable delivery did not help much either.

This all came into sharp focus for me after a friend told me that she did not believe in hell, and she was not crazy about this God thing either. Of course, I immediately began to formulate a thorough reply about how a good God could allow people to choose hell for themselves. Before I got the chance to deliver it, however, she told me *why* she didn't believe in hell. As she spoke, I realized, to my shock, that my logical argument would never change her perspective.

She described what it was like to be a little girl at the funeral of her beloved grandfather. She felt so sad and missed him so much, only to have that grief deepened when people at the church told her that her grandfather was probably in hell! Setting aside the fact that one ought not give up hope of a last-minute conversion, we should definitely never tell a grieving little girl her grandfather is damned.

I discovered that no matter how clever or thorough an argument I put together, it was clear to me that it wouldn't help my friend. She didn't have a problem with the logic of hell, or of

Christianity, for that matter. She had a deep spiritual wound that blocked her from being open to logical explanations. It might be easy to tell myself that I'm not responsible for whether or not she is open, or that I only have to make the case and leave the rest up to God. But couldn't God be calling me to be sensitive to the barriers and wounds of those with whom I am sharing the faith? Explanations are great, but only for the person actually ready to receive them.

A More Personal Way

Ultimately, events, experts, or explanations fail to accomplish the most fundamental aspect of evangelization: the personal witness and one-on-one friendship that help people encounter Jesus Christ.

As Pope St. Paul VI famously stated in his apostolic exhortation, *Evangelii Nuntiandi*, "Modern man listens more willingly to witnesses than to teachers, and if he does listen to teachers, it is because they are witnesses" (41). Or as St. Paul wrote, "With such affection for you, we were determined to share with you not only the gospel of God, but our very selves as well, so dearly beloved had you become to us" (1 Thessalonians 2:8). Are we willing to share "our very selves" with people, allowing them to become "dearly beloved"? Are we modeling for others the joy and peace of a spiritually fruitful life? Are others drawn to the Lord when they see us? We must ask ourselves if we are the kind of witnesses spoken of by Pope St. Paul VI and St. Paul.

Once we make this kind of warm friendship our focal point, the three Es become less a false promise and more a true support for evangelization. Just look at what the apostles accomplished moving forth from Pentecost, the birthday of the Church. In the Acts of the Apostles, chapter 2, we read that when Peter (the expert) got up to teach the history of Jesus (the explanation) at the feast of Pentecost (the event), three thousand were baptized that very day. Peter's preaching was then followed up by the more intimate ongoing lifestyle of discipleship.

> Every day they devoted themselves to meeting together
> in the temple area and to breaking bread in their homes.
> . . . And every day the Lord added to their number those
> who were being saved. (Acts 2:46, 47)

And so in the opening days of the Church, we see the three Es contributing to, but not completing, the larger process of conversion, a process confirmed and strengthened as new believers gathered together for fellowship in the temple and in their homes.

New Perspective

The more intimate approach of personal witness reveals just how complicated the process of conversion can be. People are messy and so is their faith journey. It often doesn't follow straight, clear, and convenient lines. In order to share the joy of the gospel, we need to walk with them in the midst of their highs and lows. We need to make ourselves available to them as Jesus did, perhaps even for years.

Jesus' strategy was amazingly simple. Sure, he spoke and taught in the temple area at times. He had big revivals with five thousand people on occasion, yet he knew that it was not primarily these experiences that would send his message to the ends of the earth. It was the intimate moments he had with his apostles. It was his time alone with Nicodemus, the woman at the well, or with Martha, Mary, and Lazarus. It was the profound witness of his quiet, holy, and loving presence that inspired people to follow him. If we really want to build the kingdom of God, we must also carry his quiet, holy, and loving presence to others.

Ultimately, no one will ever be set free to receive the joy of the gospel by an event, an expert, or an explanation. People will only ever truly experience healing and hope by meeting God in the person of Jesus Christ. As we consider how best to invite people to such a meeting, we may want to evaluate our own approach to evangelization. Where do we want to put our efforts? Do we want to lean so heavily on the three Es, or do we want to open ourselves up to better carry Christ's presence wherever we go? Growing in the fruits of the Holy Spirit will help us make this transition. In the next chapter, we'll begin our exploration of these fruits and their impact on the work of helping people move toward a personal encounter and ongoing relationship with Jesus.

Questions to Bring to Prayer

1. In what ways do I already have a close relationship with Jesus? In what ways could my relationship with him become closer?

2. What is my attitude toward the Church today? Do I believe that it is capable of growth and renewal right now? Why or why not?

3. Who in my life has had the greatest impact on my faith journey? Whose faith journey might God be calling me to better support?

Dear Jesus, thank you so much for being faithful to your Church in every generation, even when we fail at times to be faithful to you. Thank you for renewing a passion among your people to share the gospel and your very self with a world in need. Please give us more than strategies; give us a renewed outpouring of grace in your Spirit, that we might become more like you, for the salvation of souls and the glory of the kingdom. Amen.

CHAPTER 2

Discovering the Fruit of the Spirit

In the Gospel of Matthew, Jesus tells a story about a sower who freely cast seeds on the ground, some of which never take root. Other seeds land on rocky ground but grow only a little before dying. Still other seed grow a great deal before weeds choke them. Lastly, some seeds produce a bountiful harvest, thirty, sixty, or a hundredfold (see Matthew 13:1-23). This parable, with its emphasis on growth and fruitfulness, captures the theme of this book and is the source of its title.

The parable of the talents in the Gospel of Matthew also addresses the theme of growth and fruitfulness but from a different perspective. A master goes away on a long journey, entrusting different portions of his fortune to three servants until his return. Two of the three invest the money and double it. The third buries his treasure and reaps no profit for his master. When the master returns, he praises the first two servants for their faithfulness. He condemns the third for wasting the opportunity before him (see Matthew 25:14-30).

So what is the fruit in the first parable? What are these talents in the second? There seem to be two common candidates we could explore for these. The first is that of personal holiness and the second is the making of new converts to the faith. Which would you say you prefer?

Christians have faced this question throughout history. What is more important? Should I focus more on personal godliness, or should I focus more on leading others to Jesus? Should I primarily concern myself with the Great Commandment, to "love the Lord, your God, with all your heart, with all your soul, and with all your mind" (Matthew 22:37)? Or should I primarily concern myself with the Great Commission, to "make disciples of all nations" (28:19)?

As with so many aspects of Christian life, the truth rests not in an either-or proposition but in a both-and. Far from being mutually exclusive, these two demands are mutually dependent on each other. If we are going to grow in holiness, does that not require that we do all God has commanded us to do, including sharing the gospel with others? Likewise, if we strive to share the gospel with others through our words but not through our holy example, are we not frauds who do more harm than good?

Perhaps Christian communities today and throughout history have erred in overemphasizing one side or the other. The truth is that many of us probably do the same at different stages of our own faith journey. That's okay. We have a tremendously patient and generous God who understands our weaknesses and grants us so many opportunities to keep growing. Holiness and evangelization are different sides of the same coin. The more we grow in one, the more we must grow in the other. In this book, we will explore how growth in the fruits can close the gap by contributing to success in both of these calls upon us.

For My Spirit Lives in You . . .

In the Gospel of John, Jesus tells his apostles that what they have seen him do, they also will do, and greater works still (see John 14:12). This is a daunting promise, but Jesus goes on to tell them that it will be possible through the Holy Spirit, who will come to them and be with them always. In effect, the Holy Spirit activates them for mission. He does the same for us as well.

If you have been baptized, then the Holy Spirit is dwelling within you. The more you pray and open yourself up to the inner life of the Holy Spirit, the more he will bear the fruit of holiness in your life. He is gentle and will not push you, but he will bring you along if you let him, helping you grow in holiness through the fruits of the Spirit and leading you to bring the gospel to others.

In St. Paul's Letter to the Galatians, he describes nine specific fruits of the Holy Spirit: "love, joy, peace, patience, kindness, goodness, faithfulness, gentleness, self-control (Galatians 5:22-23, RSVCE). I've always thought it interesting that these are not referred to as gifts but as fruit. The Acts of the Apostles offers quite a few examples of the *gifts* of the Spirit, such as prophecy, healing, miracles, and discernment of spirits. These enable the disciples, filled with the Spirit, to testify to God's presence as these gifts are activated. The fruits of the Spirit, on the other hand, do not immediately pop up in a disciple's life—they grow over time, slowly yielding their harvest. When I was younger, I worked on an organic apple orchard. Depending on the variety of apple, it could easily take a decade for a seed to grow into a mature tree capable of bearing fruit.

Also, a funny thing about fruit trees is that taking care of the fruit itself is not the most important task. The most important task is taking care of the *tree*. A healthy tree will naturally bear good fruit in season. An unhealthy tree will not. If a tree starts to bear unhealthy fruit, no amount of cleaning, polishing, or treating the bad fruit will make it into good fruit. At best, you might be able to salvage a little of the bad fruit to use in pies. Good fruit is a by-product. It is the natural consequence of a good tree. Ultimately, the only way to turn things around when a tree produces unhealthy fruit is to take better care of the tree.

The fruits of the Spirit are also a by-product. The "tree," if you will, must be healthy. In other words, we will never develop the spiritual fruit of joy, for example, simply by trying really hard or by thinking joyful thoughts. The fruits are the supernatural consequence of a growing relationship with Christ and his Spirit.

Let me say that again. The fruits of the Spirit cannot be gained through hard work or the power of positive thinking. Without the Spirit, the best we might attain is an aptitude for pretending to possess a particular fruit. Yet even this approach will fail us in time. Cracks will start to show under the strain of our effort. No, the fruits are not so much a good thing that we do but, rather, a good thing that God does within us. They are the supernatural consequence of prayer and intimacy with him.

It is important that we keep this in mind if the fruits of the Spirit are to play an important role in evangelization. It will do us no good to struggle and strive to develop fruits on our own. We can work to remove impediments, and we can make ourselves more available to God, but he is the One who brings about the change. We are simply inviting God to do within us the good work he already wants to do. We pray not only that these fruits might grow but also that we might understand the change that God is bringing about in us. As we grow in the fruits of the Spirit, we pray that we might know how we can use them to better serve those who are far from God.

I think we are meant to develop an attraction to and a hungering for the fruits of the Spirit. Pause for a moment, and ask yourself which of these fruits are most lacking in your life: love, joy, peace, patience, kindness, goodness, faithfulness, gentleness, or self-control? Ultimately, they are all interconnected, so it is hard to grow in one of them without also growing in the others, but it still helps to hunger for one or more in particular. Foster that longing. Crave that fruit! The more we crave it and pray for it, the more God will satisfy us.

But wait. It gets better. When we develop a longing for the fruits and begin to grow in them, the people in our lives who are far from Jesus take notice. Are you generally short on patience? As you begin to bear that fruit, those who know you will say to themselves, "What is *that*?!" They will go on to say, "I want that!" As you think about the fruits most lacking in your life, you might ask yourself which fruits people most need to see in you, especially those people in your life who are far from Jesus.

Exploring Each Fruit

Growing in the fruits of the Spirit can change everything. In upcoming chapters, we will take an in-depth look at each fruit of the Spirit, how to live out that fruit, and how doing so transforms us. Also, we will consider how each fruit enables us to better share our faith with those who are far from God. In some cases, growing in a particular fruit might influence the way people far from God perceive us. In other cases, a particular fruit might change our hearts, influencing the way we think and act toward others.

Each chapter will consider a key point geared to helping us develop the fruit in our lives. Remember, there is nothing we can do to force this growth on our own. However, there is plenty we can do to remove the barriers we have inside us. This key point should help you unlock your own potential for growth. Please don't think of it as the only official way to unlock the growth, though. It's only one way. There may well be more or even better ways out there.

Ultimately, growing in the fruits of the Spirit should prepare us to better invite people to meet Jesus. Maybe we do this through Alpha or another evangelizing initiative. Maybe we do it through coffee dates with friends. Please don't tell yourself, "I just need to take these classes, and read these books. Then—maybe in twelve years when I've finished all that preparation—maybe then I will finally be ready to try a little bit of evangelization." Instead, decide with me now that you are going to try to live a more invitational lifestyle even while you are still reading this book. We need to live out both personal holiness and evangelization in the Christian life.

Descriptive, Not Prescriptive

There is nothing magic or formulaic about what I'm sharing. There is no guarantee that the people in our lives will be irresistibly drawn to conversion simply because we have changed. After all, they are free human persons with unique and unrepeatable dignity. They can choose to accept or reject God. And they can certainly reject you, even if you do everything right. As we grow in the fruits of the Spirit, however, we become a support, rather than a barrier, to those encountering the Lord.

Keep in mind too that none of us, as we grow in the Spirit, are carbon copies of each other. When I first began working on this project, I thought of the fruits as a kind of blueprint for becoming disciple makers. Then a friend of mine spoke to me about the way plants grow in a garden—a little wild and free, twisting and shifting where they will. This is good; it creates a pleasing effect. If every rosebush were identical to every other, how boring that would be! Instead, each grows freely but follows the same patterns and rules for development. There is a beauty and unity within their diversity. Similarly, the fruits of the Spirit will grow in each one of us according to a common pattern, though not bound by rigid rules that make us exactly alike.

It is my hope that this book will help to stir up new conversations and discoveries around the role of the fruits in the work of evangelization. In the next chapter, we will kick things off with the first and greatest of the fruits, the gateway for every other good thing we want to see happen within us. I bet you already guessed it! "The greatest of these is love" (1 Corinthians 13:13).

Questions to Bring to Prayer

1. We have explored the tendency for Christians to over-emphasize or to focus more of their energy either on personal holiness or on sharing their faith with others. Which of these two approaches currently receives more of your attention? Are you happy with how much effort you put into each? Why or why not?

2. The Scriptures refer to the fruits as being "of the Spirit" (Galatians 5:22). On a scale of one to ten, how comfortable are you with praying to and opening yourself up to the Holy Spirit? Why?

3. As you think about each of the fruits mentioned in this chapter, which one do you most hunger for in your own life: love, joy, peace, patience, kindness, goodness, faithfulness, gentleness, or self-control?

God, give us today a deep hunger for the fruits of your Spirit. Fill us with a passion to cooperate with your grace to become more like you. Then, unleash us into relationships with those who are farthest from you, that they might encounter your presence within us and come to know the joy of Jesus. Amen.

CHAPTER 3

Love

If I speak in human and angelic tongues but do not have love, I am a resounding gong or a clashing cymbal. (1 Corinthians 13:1)

A few years ago, when I was traveling extensively for work, I had a conversation with my coworker, John, about the toll travel can take on our relationships with our wives. Seeing my struggle, John shared a great suggestion. He said that whenever he travels, he leaves love letters at home for his wife. I thought that was a fantastic idea, so I started leaving short notes for my wife before each trip.

For the first few months, this went great . . . until the day I took a trip to Dallas, Texas. On the day of travel, I got up early in the morning to make the kids' lunches, write out bus transportation notes for their teachers, and leave a love letter for my beloved, Hollie. Several hours later, I called her from Dallas to ask if she had found her letter.

She said, "What? No, I haven't seen it."

"Oh," I responded. "It should be on the kitchen counter in a blank envelope." There was a very long pause . . .

"Umm, Josh," she said. "There is no love letter on the counter . . . but it looks like Michael forgot to take his bus note into school this morning . . ." That's right, everybody.

You guessed it. My son picked up the love letter I wrote to my wife and gave it to his teacher! A few hours later, Michael got home from school with a frantic look on his face. "Mommy, that note you gave me . . . My teacher said I was *not* supposed to give it to *her*!"

Thankfully, there was nothing too intense in there, and fortunately, Michael was only eight years old at the time. Had he been a teenager, he probably would have been scarred for life.

What Is Love, Really?

Love is the cornerstone of all the fruits of the Spirit. When we strive to practice the fruit of love in our lives, we need to make sure we have the right messaging for the specific person we want to reach. God-given, authentic love has the capacity to transform the way we relate to and experience those far from God and the way they experience us. Getting this messaging right begins with taking a good hard look at our motives. Why do we want to evangelize? When the spiritual fruit of love is at work, it acts as a check on us, holding us accountable so that we pursue evangelization for the right reasons.

It goes without saying that the worst possible motive for sharing the good news would be to build up our own ego. There is no book in heaven keeping track of how many people you have convinced to follow Christ. There is no special door prize at the pearly gates based on your tier of performance. Yet there will be times when the enemy of our souls will attempt to deceive us, when he will try to trick us into making the mission of the gospel all about us rather than those we are called to love and serve.

One approach the enemy takes in this regard is to lead us to neglect our relationship with Jesus. We hear a whispering in our ears: *Look at all the good work you are accomplishing in bringing souls to him. What need do you have for prayer and time with God?* In its vilest form, we might even be tempted to neglect the moral life as a concession for all our hard work for the mission. Neglecting prayer and devotion and turning aside from morally right conduct lead us away from the fullness of life found only in deep, intimate relationship with Jesus.

We also need to guard against the desire to be right. Have you ever had an argument with someone over a bit of mindless trivia? Who was the actor in that old movie, or which artist sings that great new song? (Today, we can just turn the debate over to Google and let the gloating begin.) There is nothing wrong with this playful competitiveness when it comes to mindless trivia, but there is when it comes to sharing the gospel. We need to guard against the unhealthy desire to win faith-related arguments, especially with those who are far from God.

This can be tough for some of us. We take the time to train, to study, and to grasp the roles of logic and reason in the life of faith. We then falsely conclude that it is righteous or holy to crush others' arguments if they disagree. It is not. Think first about the person you want to convince. It is hard enough for someone to come to Christ. Do we need to make it harder by forcing them to swallow their pride and admit we won an argument? If we really want to convince our friends to follow

Jesus, one of the worst approaches we can take is to create a situation in which we might say, "I told you so."

Finally, here's a false motive that can hit pretty close to home for many of us: evangelizing in order to bring people to church because we don't want our churches to close. Let me say that again. We should not try to convince people to come to church so that our churches won't close. Ultimately, this is selfish and inward focused. A friend of mine has referred to it as spiritual vampirism, or getting fresh blood. I understand why this can be a temptation, though. Perhaps some of you worship in the same church building as your parents, and maybe even your grandparents and great-grandparents. As the Church goes through this difficult season of shifting cultural dynamics, we can be tempted to rush out and try to bring in a bunch of new people so that we can keep the legacy alive.

Don't get me wrong. We all want to be part of something that is growing rather than dying. It is good that we love our churches, and as a secondary motivation, trying to keep them open is fine. The only appropriate reason to evangelize, however, is love—to bring people to Jesus, not to preserve our church buildings. We are enabled by the Spirit to bear the fruit of love and to extend that love to each person we encounter. Genuine love leads us to want the best for others.

Discovering the Lovability of Others

I heard about a man who attended Alpha and, as he learned to pray, began to experience profound connections to God. One week, he came back to his Alpha meeting worried that there might be something wrong with him. He told his Alpha table that he was standing in line at the post office when, all of a sudden, he felt an overwhelming sense of love for the man in front of him! He said he had never met the person before and knew nothing about him. "Is this normal?!" he asked with concern.

Maybe these days it is not, but what if it could be? This is the kind of love God feels for us all the time. As we grow in his Spirit, he may enable us to experience a little more of the love that flows through him all the time. Pause for a moment, and think of someone in your life you find easy to forget or ignore. You might have to work at it for a minute, but please wrestle with this until someone comes to mind. This is the person you might be polite to at a party, but at the same time, you find yourself glancing around for someone whose company you enjoy more. Can you picture this person? I'll wait . . . Got him? Good.

Now imagine for a moment what it might be like to see that person through God's eyes. Think about the fact that God finds this person infinitely interesting and lovable. Think about the way God watched his mother cry tears of joy as she held him in her arms for the first time. Think about the way this person's face would look in a moment of celebration or discouragement. Imagine what hopes and dreams, or at least what potential, is present within this individual that we think so dull. Consider what that person might someday be like in his heavenly state, glimmering, and vibrant with life and celestial beauty. This is just a splash of how God sees this person all the time.

Sharing Faith through Love

Jesus challenges us to love our enemies and to be good to those who hate us (see Matthew 5:44). This kind of heroic love doesn't come naturally. It is superhuman and is possible only through God's grace within us. As we become good friends with people who are far from God, they should see a difference in the way we love them compared to the way many others do. Not that we are weird or overly showy, making people uncomfortable! Rather, we are persistent, generous, and not easily shaken by disappointments.

When you consider the people in your life who are far from Jesus, would they say that there is something unique about the way you treat them? Maybe they wouldn't call it love, but would they say that you are especially attentive, generous, and genuinely interested in them? Again, not that they experience you as over-the-top, but as comforting and reassuring. Your friendship should be constant and reliable whether or not it's returned. If we settle for treating others only as well as anyone else, why would that attract anyone to Christianity?

I think Jesus did some of his best work in intimate settings of one to three people. The nearness of his presence radically transformed people. St. Teresa of Calcutta was a woman who clearly felt called to love as Jesus loved, and as a result, she had an enormous impact on our world. A young woman who spoke with her said that during the time the two of them were together, she felt as though she had 100 percent of Mother

Teresa's attention. It felt, for those few moments, as if she and Mother Teresa were the only two people in the universe.

I believe Jesus is inviting his disciples to practice that kind of loving attentiveness. In order to serve others well in this way, our love must be genuine. We must be transformed. If we try to fake or pretend our way through loving as Mother Teresa loved, the effort will exhaust us, and the cracks will show. Most people can spot a faker pretty quickly—they can tell when they're being used or when they're being loved for their own sake. Imagine, therefore, the impact on others when you allow yourself to grow in the love that is the fruit of the Holy Spirit.

A Key to Love

As with all the fruits, you can't develop love simply by trying hard or thinking positive thoughts. This transformation comes about through a deep, intimate connection with Christ's Spirit. There is nothing we can do to earn the fruit of love, but I do believe there is something we can do to properly dispose ourselves to it.

Just as those first disciples of Jesus needed time alone with him, so do we. The more time we spend with God in prayer, in the quiet of his presence, the more his love is free to work its way through us. This time should be set apart, not haphazard or occasional. My wife and I could easily sit next to each other for hours in front of a TV. Months of this might not bring us as close to one another as one afternoon spent in conversation and real effort to grow together as a married couple.

The importance of having a dedicated, regular, daily time in prayer became especially real for me a few years ago. I was attending an evening of praise and Adoration during a large conference in Cincinnati. As I knelt in the presence of God, I found myself beginning to feel distracted by all the upcoming events I had to plan and the expectations to succeed that I had imposed on myself. I thought of my call to care for my family, to love my wife well, and to raise our children in holiness and righteousness. There were the burdens of my job, my neighborhood, and my church community. I thought about all the long nights and early mornings that might be demanded of me. I felt so overwhelmed! In a moment of raw emotion, I cried out to God, "I don't have enough love to do this! God, I don't love *you* enough to serve your people the way you are calling me. Please, help me." Then, I stayed in that uncomfortable place and waited upon the Lord.

Slowly but surely, I began to feel his presence warming my heart. I felt peace and God's reassurance telling me that he would provide the grace I needed.

When we pray to God, he always answers us. Sometimes he lets us feel the warmth of his nearness as I did that day, and sometimes he does not. Yet we know he always hears and answers us in his own way. If you feel heavy and worn down, if you feel you do not have enough love to be the woman or the man that God is calling you to be, go and be alone in his presence. Return as often as you can, that he might fill you afresh with his presence.

Questions to Bring to Prayer

1. In this chapter, we explored several possible false motives for sharing the message of the gospel with the people in our lives. Which do you feel you most need to be on guard against?

2. Ask for God's eyes to see the lovability of others. Think about two or three people in your life with whom you are not particularly close. Can you ask God in prayer to reveal to you a little of what he finds so unique and lovable about them?

3. In this chapter, we also discussed the loving attentiveness practiced by Jesus and by Mother Teresa. When in your life have you experienced someone listening to you with profound attentiveness? What was it like? Do you think you could practice that kind of attentiveness with others?

Heavenly Father, please come and pour your presence upon each of us. Just as you love us, so fill us also with love, that we might be drawn more closely to you and better serve those you have entrusted to our care. This we ask for the salvation of souls and the glory of your kingdom, with the Holy Spirit, in Jesus' name. Amen.

CHAPTER 4

Joy

I have told you this so that my joy may be in you and your joy may be complete. (John 15:11)

Christians are called to be models of joy to the world, affirming by our conduct that we serve a good and loving God. My brother, Danny, told me a pretty funny story about getting to work one morning on an Ash Wednesday. He ran into a coworker of his and saw that she had ashes on her forehead. He said, "Oh, I see your ashes. Are you a Christian too?"

"Leave me alone," she said, grimacing. "I'm fasting today, and I am *not* in a good mood about it!"

Yikes!

As Christians, we have the single greatest news in all of human history. God the Son became a man to reveal to us the love of his Father. He died for our sins and rose from the dead to set us free. He returned to the Father to send us his Holy Spirit, here and now. We have before us a life of love and purpose on earth, followed by an eternity of blissful, loving intimacy with the Lord of the universe. This gospel is good news! Even on a natural level, it seems we ought to live in a state of constant joy . . . and yet often we do not.

The prophet Isaiah warns against declaring a fast in order to seek the Lord's favor, only to end up bickering and quarreling (see Isaiah 58:3-4). Sometimes when we suffer even a self-inflicted difficulty, we quickly lose a sense of the good things that God has done. But St. Paul says, "Rejoice in the Lord always. I shall say it again: rejoice!" (Philippians 4:4). Yet more often we ponder how this life is like a vale of tears, as if earthly life is only something to be endured. What is happening here, and what can we do about it?

My first job in Church ministry was as director of evangelization for St. Michael Parish in Exeter, New Hampshire. It was so easy for me to feel joyful there. I had meaningful work. I had freedom to try new things and permission to make mistakes. I had the opportunity to encounter all kinds of amazing cutting-edge tools and resources for serving the Church. I even had a faith community who welcomed this twenty-three-year-old kid who hoped he had something worth sharing.

Those three years in Exeter were some of the most meaningful ever. I married the love of my life while there. I held my newborn daughter in my arms for the first time. I developed friendships with other hopeful dreamers also committed to building God's kingdom here and now. How could I *not* feel joyful?

Then, after the third year in New Hampshire, my wife and I decided to move back to Dayton, Ohio, to be closer to family. I took a job as a business manager at a local law firm. At the time, I was praying about a switch from ministry to law school, and I thought this would help me discover if law was a good fit. It turned out to be very helpful because it was definitely not a good fit.

Each day at the firm, new people who had been accused of a crime, were getting divorced, or were fighting over custody of their children came through our doors. Whatever had brought them to us, it was invariably leaving them spiritually broken. Sadly, all we could do was minister to their legal needs. This is not meant as a criticism of anyone in the legal world. We need Christian men and women striving for goodness there.

The president of the law firm was one such Christian man, but I experienced the overall culture of the justice system as absolutely toxic. I met too many attorneys, court employees, and paralegals who were jaded and cynical. Worst of all, I discovered that I too was becoming cynical. Rather than changing this toxic culture in which I was called to be salt and light, I was allowing it to change me. I who had felt so alive just six months earlier, in ministry, now felt trapped.

Even worse, I didn't feel that I was being a good provider for my growing family. When our son was born that winter, the four of us moved into a cramped apartment in a not-so-nice part of town. We had to get a cat to keep the mice and rats from invading our home. I felt depressed and helpless. I began taking a longer route into work most mornings so that at least I could see the trees and fields outside the car window. One morning as I drove, a song came on the radio about wanting God to calm the storm of life, but choosing to praise him even if he didn't. I wept.

What Is Joy, Really?

When I was working for that law firm, was I practicing a life of Christian joy? No, certainly not. That's an easy one, but here's a trickier question. When I was working at St. Michael Parish, was I practicing Christian joy? I don't think I was. It is easy to be happy when things in life are going just the way that you want, but that is not the same as Christian joy. Joy isn't based on our daily experiences but, rather, on the confidence we have in a loving God.

It can be tempting to seek comfort or pleasure in the hope that we will finally be happy when we have what we want. The problem is that pleasure is fleeting—we will always want more. Likewise, we have no guarantee that the comfort we have today will still be there tomorrow. St. Paul was certainly an expert in having good things given and taken away, and yet he describes his joy as being something truly beyond a merely human understanding of joy:

> I know indeed how to live in humble circumstances; I know also how to live with abundance. In every circumstance and in all things I have learned the secret of being well fed and of going hungry, of living in abundance and of being in need. I have the strength for everything through him who empowers me. (Philippians 4:12-13)

Does anybody else want that kind of joy? Whether good things or bad happen to you, you would be ready to face them. Then nothing could stop you.

When I was working at the parish, I wasn't wealthy, but I had what I needed, and I was living a faithful Christian life. God really was with me, and yet my joy had shallow roots: I had not yet been tested. Essentially, everything was going my way. But all of us, sooner or later, face suffering and adversity. It is in those moments that we can come to know the deeper meaning of Christian joy. Now, the law firm may have been a difficult circumstance, but it was a far cry from the stonings or hunger St. Paul faced. Still, God used that time to teach me something about his bottomless well of joy.

What are the high and the low seasons of your life? Some of you might have much higher highs than mine. Some of you have much lower lows. No matter the season, God speaks to us in our highs and lows, teaching us about finding our true joy in him regardless of our circumstances.

A Key to Joy

Eventually, I left that law firm to work for a parish, then a Catholic radio station and, finally, to a position with the Archdiocese of Cincinnati. I thrived there, working for the ministry of marriage and family life. Over the next several years, God began to heal my wounds from my joyless experience at the law firm. I found myself getting up in the early morning to run in the woods near our new home. As the sun came up and golden beams of light washed over the foggy land, God began speaking to my heart.

This is one of the many incredible things about being humans with embodied souls. God often speaks to us directly through our bodies. He does this sometimes in the Scriptures and at church with bread and wine. He does this in cleansing through our Baptism. But he also speaks to us at times in our daily experiences, and he spoke to me through those serene morning runs. As I ran, I found myself offering up my exercise as a kind of prayer. I began to feel something bubbling from within. My attitude was changing. I felt lighter over time. I began to look at the world in a more positive way. What I was experiencing was a key to the fruit of joy. What was bubbling up inside me was hope.

At every stage of life, we have the capacity to rediscover the power of the virtue of hope—it can always flow fresh within us. I like to think of hope as confidence in God, a certainty that wherever things are today, in him they can get better. The story of your life and my life is not ultimately a tragedy; it's a tale of redemption. If your life is pretty miserable right now, hope says it can get better. If your life is just okay, keep it coming! If your life is actually pretty amazing, why stop here?! If your life is incredible and beyond your wildest dreams, guess what? It can still get better!

Ultimately, there are only two ways that hope can end in your life. The first, of course, is to enter into eternity and your heavenly reward. Then hope will end because things will be as good as they are capable of being. The other way for hope to end is for us to give up. If we stop believing, if we stop having confidence that in God our situation can actually improve, then we might be right.

I know that some of you who are reading this have suffered terribly; perhaps some of you are still suffering right now. Maybe you are struggling with a debilitating illness or injury. Maybe death has taken your child or the love of your life. Maybe you are underemployed and desperately trying to care for your family. Maybe you have been the victim of a horrific crime. I want to plead with you to not give up hope, to not give up your confidence in God that things can get better.

Fair warning: God does not always satisfy our hope by making us feel blissfully happy here on earth. He does not always heal us, give us a dream job, or allow us to experience restitution for our victimhood. Sometimes he does. Other times, he simply sustains us, helping us find joy even as we bear our burdens. Regardless of our circumstances, God always makes a way for us to find true joy in him. He always empowers us to live as his sons and daughters in the midst of our woundedness.

When I was a boy, my grandfather organized a massive family reunion. There were meals, games, stories, and even live entertainment hosted at a beautiful lake house. He even pitched in to have special Danis family t-shirts made for the occasion. Because he has always been a very spiritual man, my grandfather also wanted a verse from Scripture prominently displayed on the t-shirts.

He gave it a lot of thought, struggling to find the right verse that summed up the reality of what it means to be a Danis. When he called in the t-shirt order, however, he must have slipped up on what he meant to say because instead of the verse he picked out, the t-shirt company put Romans 8:28 on the shirts. When the t-shirts arrived, he frowned. They looked great, except that he knew Romans 8:28 was not the verse he had requested. He couldn't remember what verse he *had* requested, but he knew it was not that.

Offering a quick prayer that the verse would not be terrible, he popped open his Bible to Romans. Boy, was he relieved when he read, "We know that all things work for good for those who love God, who are called according to his purpose" (Romans 8:28). To this day, none of us know which verse he had intended to put on the shirt. But hey! It's fine. It turns out that all things work together . . . and Romans 8:28 makes a great family verse.

When we read this Scripture passage, we can be tempted to interpret it to mean that every bad thing that happens to us is actually a good thing. I don't think that is what the Bible is saying. Instead, I think we can understand that God can take the bad things that happen, even the really bad things, and somehow realign them as tools for our betterment. I didn't enjoy the time I spent at the law firm, and yet, I can look back on it now with deep gratitude for the ways it shaped the man I have become. You may never be grateful for the loss of a loved one, but God might take your pain and use it to make you a champion for someone else. Can you choose hope today that God might grow within you the fruit of joy? Remember, this is not about willpower but, rather, about opening ourselves up to receive the grace God already wants to pour into us. Then he does the hard work of bringing about the fruit.

Sharing Faith through Joy

In the early days of the Church, many Christians died as martyrs, sometimes torn apart by wild animals. And yet, there are many accounts of Christians facing persecution and martyrdom with joyful hearts. They didn't blame their persecutors. They loved them. They died singing praises to God as they boldly faced eternity, some even with smiles on their faces.

Imagine what it must have been like to catch this spectacle for the first time. Imagine you are a Roman citizen making your way through life. You have some of the finest conveniences that society has to offer. You have plenty—not as much as some, but plenty more than you need. Yet deep down you feel an emptiness; your life seems meaningless. You aren't sad, exactly, just directionless. You find some pleasure in entertainment spectacles, but it is fleeting and always harder to enjoy the next time.

Then you see one of these spectacles that's like nothing else. You see these Christians facing death with broad, joyful grins. At first, you try to tell yourself that they are crazy. The more you wrestle with it, however, the more you know that's not true. The grin of the mad cannot be mistaken for the confident smile of a truly happy person. You know that the joy the Christians express cannot be faked. As you lie on your cot that night, you are overcome by the memory of those martyrs.

You ask yourself, "Who *were* they? What did *they* have that I do not? They faced death with more joy than I face life. I *want* that!"

Today, whatever struggles, sufferings, and even persecutions you are facing, can you embrace them with joy? I believe there is perhaps nothing more astounding to those far from God than seeing us face challenges with that mysterious joy that comes from God alone.

Questions to Bring to Prayer

1. In what seasons of your life have you found it easy to feel happy? In what seasons have you found it particularly difficult? In what ways have you grown during each of these times?

2. Can you think of any examples in your life of others who have practiced astounding joy in the midst of struggle? How did their joy affect you?

3. In this chapter, we discussed how the story of each of our lives is not a tragedy but a tale of redemption. If you believe this, how might it change the way you cope with the setbacks of life?

Dear Heavenly Father, fill us each with your joy. As we face the adversity the world offers, may we never lose sight of the hope we have in you. Not by our willpower or positive thinking but by your Spirit, please grow the fruit of joy in our lives. This we ask for the salvation of souls and the glory of your kingdom, with the Spirit, in Jesus' name. Amen.

CHAPTER 5

Peace

Peace I leave with you; my peace I give to you.
Not as the world gives do I give it to you. Do not
let your hearts be troubled or afraid. (John 14:27)

Several years ago, my uncle Brett told me of his dream to move out to the country with his family in order to raise sheep and llamas. "Llamas?!" I questioned. I had never before heard of anyone who wanted to do that. "Why do you want to raise llamas?" I asked him.

"Well, you see," he explained, "the llamas are a much more stable and confident creature than the sheep. If you have a whole flock of sheep, they can easily become spooked by the slightest disruption. They might all start to run and hurt themselves. Yet if you sprinkle in a few llamas, the sheep will be reassured and not freak out as much."

"Okay," I answered, beginning to track with him. "I guess that all makes sense, but . . . why do you want to raise sheep?"

My uncle stared down at the ground for a moment, acting as if this were a completely new question for him. He then raised his eyes to meet mine so that I could see the mischievous grin on his face. "Well, the llamas are gonna need something to do!"

Sharing Faith through Peace

If we set aside my uncle's circular logic, what he described is a great image for the role that Christians ought to play in the lives of others, especially those who are far from God. When they encounter trials, our presence should bring the reassurance and sense of safety they need. When they feel panicked and anxious, we want them to be able to recall the comfort they experience with us. They can draw strength from the peaceful presence we bring with us wherever we go. As Jesus calmed the storm, we can also bring calm into the storms of other people's lives through the fruit of peace.

But what about when our presence does not deliver peace? What about when we fail to be peaceful?

Long before I worked as a business manager at that law firm, I spent a summer in college as a temp in the legal world. The first day on the job, I noticed that several of the paralegals, young people in their twenties, were looking anxious . . . even frantic. I stopped the woman who was training me to ask her what was going on. She said they were looking for an urgently needed file that had been misplaced. As this was no concern of mine, I didn't feel any anxiety about it. I did, however, think it strange that they could become so anxious over something so small.

A few minutes later, a more distinguished man in his forties entered the office. He was wearing a tie, his shoulders were back, and he had a confident air. It turned out that he was a more experienced paralegal. I remember glancing up and thinking, "Oh, here is someone who will calm everyone down and take charge of the situation." Sure enough, he quietly asked the other paralegals why they were so concerned. Much to my surprise, I watched as all his grace and presence melted away. His shoulders hunched over, and he began to wring his hands. Far from being the most composed person in the room, he quickly became the most terrified. Now even I, who had nothing to do with the file, began to feel scared. Thankfully, they found the file a few moments later, just in time.

Looking back on that moment, I cannot help but laugh at the absurdity of it. And yet, I think it accurately depicts what happens every time we Christians fail to let the fruit of peace flourish in our lives. We become like salt that has lost its flavor. Far from preserving and seasoning the world around us, we invite others into chaos. If we really believe that Jesus Christ is the Son of God and we truly believe he was sent from the Father to make us partakers in a life of grace, then we must take seriously the growth of peace within us. So much should the fruit of peace overflow in our lives that we could rightly be called peacemakers.

What Is Peace, Really?

Throughout my childhood, the adults constantly encouraged us to pray for peace in the Middle East. It seemed as if every three months, some president, politician, or world leader was called into the Holy Land to help barter agreements. Yet what they worked to negotiate was never called peace. The word they used was *cease-fire*, a word that I, as a young boy, initially found confusing.

What *is* a cease-fire? On the surface, it looks much like peace, but don't be fooled. When two enemy forces agree to a cease-fire, it means they still consider themselves at war. They remain poised to dole out destruction on each other at any moment. To an outsider, it can seem fine, but it is volatile. The war is still raging in people's hearts. The conflict is being leashed but not resolved. It will eventually reignite. Given that it is merely being bottled up, the inevitable breakdown of a cease-fire might even be worse than the original state of hostility.

Here's the thing. I think that as Christians, we sometimes long for peace in our hearts but settle too easily for cease-fire. On the outside, we can look calm and serene, but under the surface, we are boiling, anxious, and easily disturbed. We hold onto all these tensions that somehow manage to keep one another in check, but we do not know that deep well of serenity that comes from the Father. If we really want to be that positive force of comfort to others, we cannot afford to settle on these internal cease-fires.

The image of hot coals burning quietly under a light blanket of gray ash might also help to illustrate what I mean here by cease-fire. To the casual observer, everything looks completely normal. Drop any fuel remotely close to the ash, however, and you will immediately see the blaze burst back to life. The image of a deep, deep body of water can help illustrate what I mean here when I speak of peace. No matter what storms might be raging on the surface of the water, nothing can ever disrupt that quiet serenity in the depths.

A Key to Peace

Just as we can be tempted to pursue pleasure and comfort as a false path to joy, I think we can be tempted to pursue security as a false path to peace. The world encourages us to chase security, doesn't it? We buy security devices for our front doors. We load up on insurance against damage, theft, unemployment, or the death of loved ones. We save up for retirement. None of these things are wrong, but if we think they will provide us with ultimate security, we will eventually be disappointed.

Jesus speaks about this in the story of the rich man who knocks down the walls of his barns to build larger ones for his harvest. God calls him a fool: "This night your life will be demanded of you; and the things you have prepared, to whom will they belong?" (Luke 12:20). The lesson here is that there is no safety in grabbing things and drawing them toward ourselves. The security we seek comes from somewhere else.

A real key to growing the fruit of peace in your life is surrender. In other words, we must accept that we are wholly and uncompromisingly dependent on God. We ought to look at our hopes and dreams, our possessions and our wealth, and admit that they offer no guarantees. We can never fully block ourselves from every disaster. Instead, surrender enables us to become spiritually prepared to face any disaster, so long as it be with God.

We can choose to surrender today and then realize we have to do it all over again tomorrow, the next day, and the next. We might have to keep recommitting to it, but when we do, we discover a new freedom and lightness. We accept that we are not the gods of our own lives. What used to be a source of fear or anxiety becomes just one more possibility we are prepared to face beside our Father.

This doesn't mean we live expecting disaster at any moment. Just because we *can* face anything with God does not mean we *will*. But the more we can hold earthly blessings loosely, the further we can move away from anxiety and the state of cease-fire.

It's not a coincidence that Jesus says peacemakers "will be called the children of God" (Matthew 5:9). Picture a young prince and princess running around their father's castle grounds. They can play anywhere they like; they're free and safe wherever they go. Likewise, when we know that we are sons and daughters of God, we are assured that nothing can harm our spirits. There may be disappointments and even bodily harm, but we can be fearless knowing that our spirits are safe.

Persons of Peace

The Gospel of Luke tells us that Jesus sent out seventy-two disciples in pairs (see 10:1). He told them to stay in the same house in whatever town they entered. "If a peaceful person lives there, your peace will rest on him; but if not, it will return to you" (10:6). These peaceful host families became themselves a kind of gateway for the message of Christ to their community. I think we all want to be the kind of peaceful person Jesus recommends to his disciples in this passage.

Part of the success of evangelization comes from accepting that even if we are people of peace, there are individuals we will never be able to influence. There might be a barrier preventing trust between us that is simply too significant. On the other hand, there are people we can support who are in a better position to reach those we cannot. Everyone can participate in the building of the kingdom.

And if everyone gets to participate, this should force us to ask ourselves some important questions. "For whom am I a person of peace? Is it my neighbors, coworkers, family, or my sports team or club? If I cannot think of any individual or group experiencing the peace of Christ through me, is it because I do not yet have enough peace, or is it because I do not yet have many relationships? Or is it both?"

The Three Groups on the Journey

If you can think of people for whom you are a person of peace, that's great. You have arrived! Keep up the good work, the surrender, and especially the prayer . . . that God might continue to reinforce the fruit of peace in your life. If you couldn't think of any people, you fall into one of three groups on the journey of life. The first are those who are peaceful but do not yet have meaningful relationships with others, especially with non-Christians. The second are those who have relationships with non-Christians but who lack sufficient peace for it to positively impact others. The third are those who lack both relationships and sufficient peace.

Peaceful but Not Personable

As for those of you who do not have many relationships, well, I think you probably know what you have to do. Get out there and make some more friends! Start engaging your neighbors in conversation until it would no longer be weird to invite them over. Join a new group, or get to know people better in a group to which you belong. Don't say you're too busy. Cut out those things in your life that are stopping you. Go volunteer! How can we ever hope to have a positive impact on others if we refuse to know them and be known by them? You have a special gift in your capacity for peace. Share it!

If you are an introvert, it may be difficult for you to do this with lots of people, but that's okay; God will meet you where you are. If you are an extrovert, it might be easy to get to know lots of people but difficult to go deep in friendship with any of them. Again, God will meet you where you are. Pray for grace, and God will place you in the opportunities he has to use you.

Personable but Not Peaceful

What about that second group? If you do not yet have sufficient peace, do not be afraid. Pray.

> Have no anxiety at all, but in everything, by prayer and petition, with thanksgiving, make your requests known

to God. Then the *peace* of God that surpasses all understanding will guard your hearts and minds in Christ Jesus. (Philippians 4:6-7, emphasis mine)

Perhaps you have lots of friends and associates, but you have not yet modeled peace to them in such a compelling way that they see anything different about you. Are you too easily disturbed by an unkind word from someone? Do you fear for your personal safety in the future? Do you spend an inordinate amount of time complaining and worrying about the things that are beyond your control?

Many people may initially turn to Jesus because they see him as a comforter for their many fears and anxieties. This is a good thing! Jesus is the shepherd—he offers much better security than any llamas on my uncle's sheep farm ever could. It is natural that our fear and anxiety might initially draw us toward Christ. He brings comfort in the midst of it, but then he also invites us to grow past our fear, to model peace to the other people in our lives.

Neither Peaceful nor Personable

That only leaves us with one more group. What if no one is experiencing you as a person of peace, both because you are not peaceful *and* because you do not have relationships? First, I want to encourage you because I think you probably have a lot of company. This is also the group with which I would most identify. If we are being honest, I think most of us fall into this group too much of the time. For us, it's tempting to focus on growing in peace and avoiding people until we get really good at it.

If I might humbly offer my opinion, I think we cannot afford to wait. It is too easy for us to keep coming up with excuse after excuse to avoid engaging with people. We will probably never have it all together. Sometimes I have this rosy-eyed view of myself meeting a new person and doing everything right, all the time. This is more than a little absurd. Of course we are going to keep screwing up! But maybe people will be drawn to Christ's presence within us not so much by our perfection as by our gradual improvement.

I know a young man whose wife came back to church not because he was an angel but because he was so much better than he used to be. She told me, "Yeah, he used to be angry all the time, and then he met Jesus on Alpha and started going to the parish in town. I felt like I was married to a completely different man. He wasn't perfect, but he was *better*." Maybe God is not calling us to astound people by how peaceful we are all the time. Maybe he is inviting us to astound people by how much more peaceful we are than we used to be.

Questions to Bring to Prayer

1. Was there ever a time when someone surprised you by their ability to remain peaceful in the midst of adversity? Have you ever surprised yourself by remaining peaceful?

2. In this chapter, we discussed the analogy of cease-fire as a kind of pretended peace in which everything looks peaceful on the outside. How much better would it feel inside to surrender?

3. We spoke in this chapter about persons of peace being both personable and peaceful. Which of these two qualities is easier for you? Why?

Dear Heavenly Father, please fill us with deep peace. May we remain unsatisfied by the false promises of cease-fire and instead strive to cooperate with you as you establish the fruit of peace within us. Give us the courage to surrender each day and ultimately to become the persons of peace who draw our friends, neighbors, and loved ones toward you, for the salvation of souls and the glory of your kingdom, with the Spirit, in Jesus' name. Amen.

CHAPTER 6

Patience

I was mercifully treated, so that in me, as the foremost, Christ Jesus might display all his patience as an example for those who would come to believe in him for everlasting life. (1 Timothy 1:16)

Recently, I came across a funny cartoon on social media. A man knelt at his bed for nighttime prayers. He said something like this: "Dear God, please give me patience, and when I ask for it, I do not mean I want more opportunities to grow in patience. I've had plenty of those, and they don't seem to be helping. So now, I would just like to receive actual patience!"

Yes, wouldn't that be wonderful, to wake up tomorrow morning and discover we suddenly possess the patience to meet any circumstance. However, patience, as with all the fruits, comes about not through wishful thinking but through intimacy with Christ. We will know the fruit of patience is at work in our lives when we can see that we have the ability to exercise it.

What Is Patience, Really?

Although there are several possible definitions of patience, I hope you don't mind if I am partial to my own. I like to think of patience as the ability to gracefully endure unpleasant circumstances for the present time. What do I mean? To begin, what are unpleasant circumstances? These could come in many forms. They could be self-inflicted, such as going without our favorite foods or sweets, or getting up each morning to run. Other people might impose unpleasant circumstances on us—if you've ever been on a crowded bus next to someone coughing and sneezing, you have endured an unpleasant circumstance imposed by another. A more intense unpleasant circumstance would be keeping a job in which we are unhappy because we need to support our family. Lastly, we can speak of circumstances beyond our control, such as enduring a natural disaster or being the victim of a crime.

Next, what do I mean by gracefully endure? That word—*gracefully*—is important, especially to us as Christians. To do something gracefully is to do it with poise and composure. Technically, someone who keeps a job they hate for the sake of their family is enduring. If they go home each night and drink excessively and yell at their children, they are not being patient. They lack grace. We might find their endurance admirable, but I don't think we should call it patience. It is probably not a coincidence that the term "grace" refers to how we positively conduct ourselves and to the sanctifying action of God within us that makes such positive conduct possible. To be graceful literally requires that we also be grace filled by the power of God.

The last piece of my definition refers to the idea that the circumstances are only for the present time. Built into the very idea of patience is a desire for things to improve in time and a commitment to doing our part to make that happen. We will not be on that bus or hate our job forever. We will again taste the joy of sweets and either stop running or, better still, fall in love with it so that it no longer requires patience. Even the person who is patiently surviving a natural disaster should commit to the idea that they will not spend the rest of their lives in crisis mode. Endurance without the commitment to improve the circumstance is not patience. It is the acceptance of defeat.

Some of the challenges that require our patience will not end while we are on earth. Certainly, the martyrs who endured death for Jesus were placing their patience into a commitment to the next life. And some circumstances requiring patience will be ongoing and generational, needing to be taken up again and again over the years. Social reformers working to overcome racism, for example, have endured slurs, insults, and threats in their commitment to building a better world for their children, if not for themselves. They could have kept their heads down or fled. Instead, they practiced patience, not as defeat, but as the very means of attaining the justice they sought.

Again, patience is the ability to gracefully endure unpleasant circumstances for the present time. I like this definition because I think it sets the standards that will allow the fruit of patience to grow within us. In order for Christians to truly practice patience, we must not only endure, but do so gracefully, maintaining a commitment to the vision of the better circumstance we seek.

Mary, the mother of Jesus, offers the best example of the fruit of patience at work within a person. When the angel Gabriel spoke to her and revealed God's plan, Mary understood that this pregnancy came with dire and potentially deadly consequences. Much depended on how Joseph would respond. Yet Mary trusted and waited for God to resolve the danger. If I were her, I know I would have been overcome by anxiety. She, however, committed herself to the certainty that the same God who gave her Jesus would also take care of everything she needed. As the time for delivery approached, she suffered countless hours on the road on the back of a donkey. Then she experienced labor in a stable surrounded by farm animals. She accepted each of these struggles gracefully, trusting that God was bringing about the promises he had made to her.

In his Gospel, Luke reminds us that Mary pondered in her heart the events surrounding the life of Jesus. I think this pondering helped Mary face the joys, the difficulties, and, eventually, even the death of her son with patience. Throughout Scripture, she remains a figure of grace, expectantly awaiting the promises of God. But let's not mistake her patience for passivity. During the wedding feast at Cana, for example, it is Mary who calls Jesus to action, opening the way for him to perform his first public miracle. So great is her confidence in her son that when the moment of action arrives, she recognizes and seizes it.

A Key to Patience

By now, you have observed the ways in which all of the fruits are mutually dependent upon one another. They are like trees that have the ability to cross-pollinate. In his First Letter to the Corinthians, St. Paul reminds us that "love is patient"

(13:4). Just as joy flows from hope, so hope also plays a role in the development of patience, and patience in the development of peace.

But what about patience itself? Yes, there is a special key that will open you up to receiving the fruit of patience: context—in other words, keeping things in perspective. When I was younger, I was anxious and worried all the time. I wasted many hours replaying conversations in my head and kicking myself for one thing or another that I could have said or done better. I dreaded tests and social interactions. Every single decision seemed so important, as though the very fate of my life hung in the balance.

As I have grown a little older, I have noticed something. Despite making many decisions, some good and many bad, I am still here. The things that seemed so serious, a matter of life-and-death, were really nothing but a much smaller part of a larger story. When I make mistakes, I strive to correct them. When I sin, I repent and keep going. The point is that within the simple context of more years of life experience, I have learned to not take each moment so seriously.

As we pass through our twenties, thirties, and into our sixties and so on, we grow in our ability to see things through the lens of this broader perspective. That doesn't always mean that the more experienced person is right in every circumstance. Sometimes the eighteen-year-old has greater insight into a situation than someone four times their age. It is not necessarily a matter of the number of years but of the unique insights of our experience.

Keeping an eternal perspective—seeing things in the context of God's eternal plan—will help us grow in patience. There is a wisdom that comes from examining each moment of life in light of the much larger story of what God is doing. When we keep salvation history in mind and the presence and action of the Holy Spirit in the world even today, it can feel a little silly to lose our temper when someone cuts us off in traffic. In Scripture, as well as in the Church, God has placed our individual human experience in a far grander context. Maybe tapping into this perspective and keeping it in mind can be a gateway to developing the fruit of patience.

Sharing Our Faith through Patience

In my work with Alpha and in parishes, I have met many parents who tell me, with tears in their eyes, about the begging and pleading they have done in an effort to draw their grown children back to the Church. "I don't understand!" they tell me. "I did everything I was told to do, and yet I have somehow lost them." I wish I had an easy answer for these discouraged people, but there are many layers to what they are experiencing. First, the culture has transformed dramatically over the past fifty or sixty years, and the game of Christian parenting has changed with it. What was more than sufficient preparation for a life of faith a few generations ago does not break the surface of the challenges people face today.

Second, maybe the way the Church prepared parents to pass on the faith was not as adequate as we believed. Catechism class and receiving the sacraments are essential, but maybe people in today's culture need more help in order to encounter God. My friend Ryan once came to me, flabbergasted by his experience teaching theology at a Catholic school. "Josh, my students are all doing really well in my classes," he told me. "Most of them get As, and they can give you all the right answers to the questions on the tests. Yet when I have a conversation with them, I can see that they aren't even sure God exists, much less whether or not they can have a relationship with him."

A third layer to the answer for discouraged parents of adult children might be the most painful of all. When Jesus sent his disciples out to preach the good news, he knew that some of the towns would reject his message. In such instances, he did not instruct the disciples to beg, plead, or threaten. He told them to shake off the dust and go to the next town. Certainly, Jesus hoped that the people in towns that rejected his message would come around in time, but he is also admitting a painful truth. Not everyone is going to be won over to the gospel on our terms or in our time frame.

Patience teaches us that we need to be okay with people freely taking their time. We must always be ready to share the gospel and seek better ways to do so, but we also need to be careful that we are not pushy about it or speak up at the wrong time.

This will be freeing for us as well. A patient approach reminds us that we are not the saviors of anyone. God might allow us weak, broken, and humble people to play a small part in the good that he is working in others, but let's not delude ourselves. He, through his Holy Spirit, is the main player in their journey to conversion. Patience reminds us of the context and the fact that there are several forces working toward their conversion. If you are worried about your children who have stopped going to church, remember that God has also placed other Christians in their neighborhoods, in their companies, and in the gyms where they work out. Pray not only for your children but for those others who will be called to share the gospel with them.

But How Patient Is Too Patient?

The fruit of patience can be a little tricky when it comes to the work of evangelization. On the one hand, we accept that we don't always get what we want when we want it, including the conversion of others. On the other hand, we have to guard against doing nothing for the gospel, and then claiming that we are just being patient. That's not patience; it's accepting defeat.

There is a popular saying often attributed to St. Francis of Assisi: "Preach the gospel at all times. Use words when necessary." Properly understood, there is some merit to this idea. Unfortunately, I have seen it applied in not-so-helpful ways. Rather than taking it as a challenge—that our deeds must correspond to our words—it's often used as a cop-out, implying that we need not speak about Jesus as long as our actions are Christlike.

People might be surprised to discover how often Francis of Assisi felt the need to use words, often preaching to others about the gospel. He sent members of his community to preach regularly throughout all of Italy. So enthusiastic was Francis about words that he even risked martyrdom by traveling to the Middle East and preaching to the sultan. Like Francis, we want our actions to reflect our faith, but also, like Francis, we want to "use words" at the right time and in the right ways.

We need to be patient with people and work to discern the appropriate times and places that God ordains. Patience requires that we never bully or manipulate someone. We allow them to say no, but we are also attentive to the next occasion to gracefully and appropriately share about Jesus. I know, all this waiting can sometimes be exhausting, but if conversion is to be real, it cannot be forced.

There is good news, though. God gives us one area in which we don't have to practice patience, and we should leverage it. We are not required to wait patiently at all when it comes to prayer. God encourages us to pray constantly, intensely, and intentionally for our requests. Like the man knocking on his neighbor's door after dark, seeking food for his guests (see Luke 11:5-8), God invites us to storm heaven with our prayers on behalf of those who do not know him. We know, in faith, that God always answers our prayers—not always when we want or in the way we might expect, but he does answer.

Let us overwhelm people with grace through the prayers we pray on their behalf. Then, like Mary, who knew when to act and when to ponder, let us be patient.

Questions to Bring to Prayer

1. Think of a circumstance in your life that requires patience. Have you found being patient mostly difficult or mostly easy? What lessons or spiritual gifts might God be offering you through these times when you are called to exercise patience?

2. A key to growing in patience is context—seeing the bigger picture of what God is doing. What are some big-picture things you have seen God doing lately that are worth celebrating? How is the growth of his kingdom being played out around you?

3. When it comes to sharing your experience of the gospel, would you say that you are more likely to be too patient, failing to share readily when appropriate, or to be not patient enough?

Dear Heavenly Father, work a miracle in each of us through the fruit of patience. May we endure the hardships of life with grace and confidence in you. May our patience inspire the people in our lives to long for you as the only true source of satisfaction. Challenge us to be patient with other people but also to storm heaven with our prayers, for the salvation of souls and the glory of your kingdom, with the Spirit, in Jesus' name. Amen.

CHAPTER 7

Kindness

Whatever you did for one of these least brothers of mine, you did for me. (Matthew 25:40)

If you have never read Dr. Gary Chapman's book, *The 5 Love Languages*, I highly encourage you to look into it. He has quantified the most common ways in which people prefer to both show and receive love from others: words of affirmation, quality time, receiving gifts, acts of service, and physical touch. The book's insights greatly helped me in what it revealed about my interactions with others, especially my wife. For example, my love languages, from most important to least, are touch, words of affirmation, quality time, gifts, and service. My wife's love languages, in order, are service, gifts, quality time, words of affirmation, and touch. In case you didn't notice, my wife's love languages are the exact . . . opposite . . . of mine. So yeah, we have gained incredible insight into what it means to love each other well.

Acts of service do not always come naturally to me, and I have a long way to go. For Harold Graczyk, my father-in-law, however, this was something that just flowed out of him. I think his first love language must have been acts of service. When Hollie and I first got married, I confess that I used to feel threatened by Harold's propensity to serve. For crying out loud, he once cleaned out my entire garage! The next time he came to visit, I made sure to have the garage spotless, and yet he *still* found ways to improve it.

I think this made me feel threatened because I saw his acts of service as an attempt to say, "Hey, you cannot really take care of my daughter, so I have to do it for you." After I discovered the love languages, I realized that I had him all wrong. He wasn't being kind to make a statement. He was being kind because that is who he was. He loved his daughter, and he loved *me*. The best way he knew to show us was by serving in ways small and large, even if that meant cleaning out our garage.

What Is Kindness, Really?

True acts of kindness are not done out of fear or obligation, or out of a desire to receive thanks or to motivate someone to do something for us. Rather, they simply flow out of a person.

I think that most people who are kind almost never know that they are. Perhaps they are naturally kind, or perhaps they have achieved tremendous growth in the fruit. It has become their natural state, and they might even assume that it's everyone's natural state. Those who are kind tend to insist that they get more out of performing kind acts than the people who are receiving their kindness. We would think them crazy, except that the experience is so universal. What's going on here? It is as though acts of charity tap so deeply into who we are called to be as persons that when we perform an unselfish act, we feel grateful to the people who gave us the opportunity to serve them.

The Church has a long history of performing acts of kindness. Christians played essential roles in the development of the hospital and university systems, and the Church has had a hand in a staggering number of social benefits throughout the last two thousand years. We are obsessive about recognizing the dignity of every single human being and working to ensure that dignity is respected. Our missions all over the world not only bring the gospel to many but also work to meet the physical needs of those who are poor and suffering. At our best, we are truly kind, living up to the call to love our neighbors as ourselves.

My father, Mark Danis, left the corporate world a few years ago to begin serving the poor full-time with the Society of St. Vincent de Paul. In his work, he interacts with hundreds of kindhearted volunteers trying to do their part. Some of them come once or twice a year to help in a limited capacity. Those who have the greatest impact, however, adopt a steady cadence of serving on a monthly or even weekly basis.

Occasional volunteer service is great, and often it's all that busy people can manage. My point here, however, is simply this: to perform single instances of kindness on an occasional basis is to dabble in the fruit of kindness. To develop a committed, lifelong cadence is to make a gift of your very self. It is in those moments that the fruit of kindness can best take root and grow.

Extraordinary Kindness

Back in college, I went on a service mission to New York City. I worked with the Missionaries of Charity, a group of religious sisters founded by St. Teresa of Calcutta. When I first heard that the Missionaries of Charity were serving in the United States, I think I laughed out loud. Sure, it made sense to me that they would support the poorest of the poor in a place like Calcutta, but why would they come to serve in the richest nation in the world?

I knew that there was poverty here, but I was humbled to discover the depths of destitution in our midst. Along with homelessness and hunger, many can experience a terrible sense of hopelessness here. This hopelessness is a form of spiritual poverty that can be more dire than physical poverty.

One day, while serving in New York City, I watched as a bitter, angry man swore and cursed at one of these religious sisters. He actually called her a wicked, evil woman *while she was serving him his lunch*! From a depth of love that amazed me, she went about serving him, completely unphased by his rudeness. I think I would have been tempted to scold him or make him apologize before I would bestow my kindness, but that was not her way. There was no string attached to the love she poured out on him, not even the string of simple human decency.

The next day, I discovered that this type of generosity, poured out over time, could have an astounding effect upon those who receive it. I went with the Missionaries of Charity to help out at their hospice for men suffering and dying from AIDS. If anyone had the right to feel bitter, angry, and justified in lashing out against the world, surely it would be these men. And yet, these men demonstrated the opposite attitude.

Many of the men had been emotionally touched by the love of the sisters. Rather than cursing them, they were deeply grateful. They were so grateful, in fact, that they seemed compelled to return the generosity. Several of the men asked how they could help and jumped at the opportunity to sweep floors and do other chores. To me, it seemed that they had been welcomed into a community of love, and they were just reveling in the chance to do their part within it.

I was overwhelmed with tears when my eyes settled on a verse of Scripture that had been inscribed on one of the walls: "The LORD gave, and the LORD has taken away; / blessed be the name of the LORD!" (Job 1:21). What on earth could lead a group of men suffering as they were to embrace such a perspective? What other than the profound kindness of other people who had given their whole lives to serving Christ in others.

A Key to Kindness

In order to cooperate with the growth of the fruit of kindness in our lives, it helps to fall in love with others. Not in a romantic sense, but as we saw in the chapter on love, in a way that allows us to really see the people around us. We need to tap into a sense of their hopes, their dreams, their fears, and their needs. When this happens, we might find ourselves beginning to root for them. We might long to see them safe, happy, and successfully living out the call God has placed in their own lives.

When this happens, kindness proves that it is not self-serving, nor is it a cold calculation about what to do to lessen human suffering in general. It becomes a specific outpouring—we couldn't stop ourselves from such kindness if we wanted to. Even when we support those who are needy by donating money, there is something more genuine, more wholesome about choosing to get to know all about the people we are serving. To say "Take my money and leave me alone" is less a matter of spiritual fruitfulness and more a matter of satisfying a guilty conscience. To say "Tell me all about these people I will be helping" demonstrates authentic kindness and helps us develop and be attentive to this fruit of the Spirit.

Sharing Our Faith through Kindness

One more cool thing about the fruit of kindness is its propensity to show up in unexpected places. There are many non-Christians, for example, who are kinder and more charitable than some Christians. This circumstance demonstrates that we Christians are not yet living up to our responsibility to become Christ to the world. But it also demonstrates that God has placed seeds of goodness in all the people of the world, something we might want to keep in mind when we share the gospel with others. I believe he has placed in all people a natural capacity for kindness.

As Christians, we ought to be accessing the supernatural capacity for self-sacrificing kindness that God gives us through grace. "No one has greater love than this, to lay down one's life for one's friends" (John 15:13). And it's true that acts of superhuman kindness can delight and astound the people of the world, leading them toward Jesus. But low-key kindness can also have an outsized impact. Some people have their first positive exposure to the faith not at church or even at Alpha but while serving side by side with Christians in providing service to the needy. When a person cooperates with the Church in raising money to care for sick children or hand out sandwiches to the homeless, she may feel a stirring in her heart that says, "This is right. This is where I belong."

Leaving a Legacy to Inspire

My father-in-law passed away a couple of years ago. He was certainly not perfect in every way. He had been a heavy drinker as a young man, before spending the last twenty-five-plus years of his life sober. He sometimes worked too hard, especially before his conversion to Christ. During the time that I knew him, however, he went to church almost every single day. He spent over an hour daily in personal prayer as well.

Despite his deep faithfulness, I never heard that he taught a religion class. I never saw him give his testimony in front of a group, though I know he did witness one-on-one quite often. At face value, he seemed to be a simple, committed, but basically unremarkable Christian . . . but that was only at face value. On the day of his funeral, approximately one thousand people showed up to pay their respects and testify to what a remarkable man he truly was.

As these people came through the line to introduce themselves, I heard story after story of those he visited while they were sick or in the hospital. I heard of men he counseled to be better husbands. I heard of someone who had been drunk and in a dangerous part of town in the middle of the night. They could think of only one person they could trust to call at that hour. Harv drove two hours through the night to save them from their situation. I heard men in their fifties to their twenties—and even teens—insist that he was the best coach they ever had. Over and over again, each said separately that he didn't just teach them hockey, but he taught them what it means to live a good life.

His best friend gave a eulogy before the funeral and shared about a time my father-in-law house-sat for him. While taking care of this friend's home and pets, do you know what else my father-in-law found time to do? *He cleaned his friend's garage!* Coaching, visiting the sick, caring for others, cleaning garages, and so many other acts of generosity were just part of the summation of who he was in Christ Jesus. I never knew, while he was alive, what an impact he was having as he practiced his quiet cadence of kindness. I can only hope to live up to a fraction of his legacy.

Questions to Bring to Prayer

1. Whose legacy of kindness is God inviting you to follow in your life?

2. Many people who perform acts of kindness on a regular basis insist that they get way more out of the act than the person who is actually receiving their kindness. Have you ever experienced this yourself? What do you think these givers are receiving? Why?

3. We have discussed developing a steady cadence of kindness. What acts of kindness has God called you to repeat on a regular basis? What acts of kindness might he be inviting you to perform more regularly?

Dear Heavenly Father, thank you for planting within each of us the seeds of the fruit of kindness. Please make us deeply generous, just as you are generous with us. May our cadence of kindness flow not from obligation or pride but, rather, out of our love for you and others. Empower the members of your Church to astound and inspire an unbelieving world through sacrificial kindness. This we ask for the salvation of souls and the glory of your kingdom, with the Holy Spirit, in Jesus' name. Amen.

CHAPTER 8

Goodness

I believe I shall see the Lord's *goodness / in the land of the living. (Psalm 27:13)*

Have you ever noticed that there are some fruits everybody likes to eat? Apples and oranges come to mind, but it's okay if you disagree. I think we can all agree, however, that grapefruit is definitely an acquired taste.

My first exposure to this fruit was as a very small boy visiting my grandparents in upstate New York. I came downstairs for breakfast one morning and poured my little bowl of Cheerios. Then I saw that my grandfather was enjoying what I thought to be the largest orange I had ever seen. Despite my begging and pleading for one of my own, he insisted that it was not what I thought it was and that I would not like it.

I was a small boy, though. I was pretty stubborn. When I finally prevailed upon him to let me try the grapefruit, I wanted so much to be able to fake liking it. In the end, I couldn't hold it together. That fruit was awful. It was somehow bitter and sour at the same time. Despite its rich floral scent, it was worse than most of the vegetables I had been forced to down as a child. I couldn't see why anyone would want to call it a fruit at all! Sometime around high school, I finally did acquire a taste for grapefruit, and I remember thinking of it as a rite of passage into adulthood, right up there with drinking coffee and learning to shave.

What Is Goodness, Really?

Goodness might very well be the grapefruit of the fruits of the Spirit: incredible and refreshing, but only after you have developed a taste for it. Many Christians describe goodness in terms of righteousness or living the moral life. This is an appropriate connection, but it doesn't tell the whole story.

When we think of objects like a car or a coffeemaker, we define their level of goodness based on whether or not they do the task for which they were created. A car can have an incredible paint job, comfortable seats, and cup holders everywhere. But if it doesn't get you from home to work and back again without breaking down, it's not a good car. That coffeemaker might fit perfectly into the color scheme of your kitchen, but if it doesn't deliver your morning caffeine, it's already in the trash. There is also an element of goodness in excelling at that which you are called to do. If I say that my brother Luke is a good runner, well, you already know that he can run fast, far, or likely both.

With this in mind, I would like to consider the fruit of goodness from the perspective of succeeding and excelling at the things we were put on this planet to do. This absolutely requires that we avoid sin, but it also requires that we discover and strive to accomplish whatever God specifically has in mind for our life's work. Think of the man who passes away at the ripe age of ninety. The number one thing he wants people to be able to say about him is that he lived a good life. This means not only that his time on earth was rich and meaningful but also that he made a positive difference in the lives of people who knew him. It strongly suggests that he lived a life worth living, a life in accord with what God placed him here to do during his many decades.

Sharing Our Faith through Goodness

Sharing our faith with those who are far from God can be tricky when it comes to the fruit of goodness. Sure, popular fruits like joy and peace draw people toward Christ right from the start, but goodness might be more of an acquired taste. If we Christians intend to attract the world to an encounter with Jesus, we need to keep in mind the negative connotations people can attach to this fruit.

It helps to be aware that in Western culture, there is a tendency to mash together several concepts under the term "goodness" in such a way that the word and the reality behind it become unappealing. Goodness can be used to mean that someone is a goody-goody, a teacher's pet. It could mean someone is a bore in social situations or that they always play it safe and do what they are told.

On the flip side, our culture has also identified all kinds of positive meanings around the concept of *badness*. We associate it with being tough, bold, adventurous, and even attractive. TV and film have sold us on the appeal of dating the bad boy or bad girl. That being said, I am yet to meet a single person who tells me they want to be married to a bad husband or a bad wife. This is because we associate the concept of badness in a married context with being selfish, unreliable, or unloving. As we continue to unpack goodness, keep in mind these strange little twists of the language because they influence people's perceptions of this fruit.

Goodness is also often associated with being judgmental. When I was teaching a Christian initiation class a few years ago for those exploring joining the Church, I was startled to discover that the students only knew the word *pious* by its negative connotation. When I spoke of piety as one of the seven gifts of the Spirit, they all frowned at me. They had only ever heard the word used sarcastically. To them, "Oh, he is *pious*!" was the same as saying, "He just thinks he's perfect and better than everyone else." If this is a widespread perception, we clearly have an uphill battle ahead of us in building the case for goodness.

To be fair, we Christians have done plenty to help feed this stereotype of being judgmental. I have seen it play out over and over again in my own life. At a stage of our development in the faith, many of us focus our energy on whether or not we seem to be becoming righteous. This is not necessarily a bad thing, but we often pair our self-concern with a temptation to look down on those who do not seem to be similarly motivated. That is a bad thing. Unlike Jesus, who refused to cast the first stone of condemnation, we often sound more like the Pharisee who thanked God that he was not like the rest of humanity. I too have been guilty of this.

So yes, this is tricky, isn't it? We really do want to excel in the moral life—not because Christianity is about living up to the expectations of the law, but because the more we grow in love, the more we ought to long to do that which is pleasing to God. I think it helps to maintain a focus on God and on *his* goodness. Many of our greatest saints in history saw themselves throughout life as terrible sinners, saved only by the grace of a loving God. They rejoiced in the freedom they had in their beloved Jesus, but they never made the mistake of considering their righteousness their own. It was always something God was doing within them. Therefore, they never compared themselves to others, only to the infinite goodness of God.

Fertilizing Goodness in Others

Would you like to help fertilize the seeds of goodness in the people around you? In my experience, there is no better way to do this than to regularly catch them in the act of doing something good. I am reminded of an incident a couple of years ago when I was helping out at a large conference. Someone was having trouble finding their way to the lost and found, so I helped them. It only took a moment, and I honestly didn't think much of it at the time. However, one of my superiors caught me in the act and praised me extensively for it.

As she lavished affirmation on me for what I thought was a pretty run-of-the-mill activity, I felt a conviction growing within me. I knew that I wasn't worthy of the level of praise I was receiving, but I also discovered that I really wanted to be worthy of it. Though slightly over-the-top, I don't think the person who encouraged me was trying to deceive or manipulate me. Like most humans, I'm pretty good at catching a fraud. No, I think she was a person of praise and profound encouragement—it came naturally to her. Maybe it was even a product of the fruit of joy at work in her life.

Regardless, I think we should all try, regularly, to catch people in the act of doing the right thing and make sure to praise them for it. Whether the actions are big or small, whether the person committing them is a Christian or not, people deserve to get caught doing something good. This will not only make them feel valued but also might deepen a hunger for goodness within them. So long as it is genuine, our affirmation will likely lead them to pursue yet more goodness. Fruit begets fruit.

A Key to Goodness

So how do we do this? How do we grow in goodness, and how do we share our goodness with others in a way that is not off-putting or perceived as being judgmental? I believe I have some encouraging news here. The very thing that enables us to grow in the fruit is the same thing that makes it more palatable for others: humility. We need to pray for and open ourselves up to receive this great gift of God.

Humility before God

When I was growing up, my parents often took us hiking in the Green Mountains of Vermont or the Adirondacks of New

York. Recalling those days brings up the image of a foggy mountain valley. Imagine that you start out early one morning from deep in the heart of a foggy valley. At first, you can only see five or six feet in front of you because the fog is so thick. Gradually, as you make progress up the trail, you reach a point at which you can see ten feet, then twenty, and so on.

The good news here is that the farther up the trail you travel, the easier it is to see the peak. The bad news is that the farther you can see, the farther you discover you still have to go! The best of us, in our pursuit of goodness, are probably the ones who know how far they still have to grow. Of course, there is also real freedom in this. Don't bother relying on your own righteousness. You don't *have* any! But don't constantly beat yourself up. God is leading you toward goodness, and humility will help you get there. All is grace.

Humility before Others

Of course, we want others to perceive our goodness as a blessing to them. We don't want them to perceive us as judgmental or good in an off-putting way. We certainly don't want the goodness of God to be something we lord over anyone. We want goodness to be shared by all. The worst-case scenario would play out along the lines of what we see mentioned in the Book of Wisdom: "Let us lie in wait for the righteous one, because he is annoying to us" (2:12).

We can take one positive step toward humility by being honest about our shortcomings. We don't need to go out of our way to talk about them, but when someone brings them up, we ought not be defensive but, rather, freely admit our need for grace. Of course, we shouldn't do so in a manner that suggests moral failings are no big deal. Rather, we should humbly admit to the ways we are definitely far from perfect but be clear that we are still striving.

It can even be helpful to speak freely about our minor flaws as well. If someone calls you a klutz, go ahead and admit to it without reservation. This openness can be endearing and can even lead to moments of great honesty through which God speaks to your accusers, especially if they are far from him. And if others see that we are not falsely humble but truly aware of our shortcomings, they might see what goodness we do have as a positive trait, something endearing rather than intimidating.

Should We Never Correct Others?

With all this emphasis on humility, you might wonder if it's ever appropriate to tell others that what they are doing is wrong. No doubt, there are a few Christians who would claim that we should correct every person we ever see sinning, regardless of whether or not we have a relationship with them. I suppose there are also Christians who would claim that we should never correct anyone, regardless of how deep our relationship is. I don't claim to be an expert here, but in an effort to apply the fruits of the Spirit to evangelization, I'd like to explore a few principles.

It goes without saying that if we have direct moral authority over someone, we not only have the right but also the duty and responsibility to instruct and correct them. Obviously, our children fall into this category, at least before they are adults. Once they become adults, they are free agents, and no amount of pushing and prodding from us is likely to be fruitful if they have turned away from the Lord. We may be free at times to provide input, but they are no longer under our authority and will make their own choices.

A second category of people we may correct are those individuals who directly represent us, such as an employee or business partner who is empowered to speak for us. Should they conduct themselves in a way that is unbecoming, especially in a moral matter, you should absolutely challenge them. Someone who represents you politically, such as an elected official, for example, is also subject to your correction.

A third category includes anyone with whom you have a voluntary relationship of mutual accountability. Spouses and siblings can fall into this group, but it also includes fellow Christians alongside whom you worship and pray. Tragically, too few Christians today know each other well enough to establish a level of intimacy that will allow them to hold each other accountable. When healthy, this type of accountability in a relationship can be about much more than avoiding sin. We can also hold one another accountable to prayer, to commitments, and even to our goals in service to the kingdom. We should also encourage and pray for one another as well.

When it comes to those far from God, I think our motivation should not be to condemn but to encourage. If we condemn them, they are likely to ignore us anyway. After we have established a relationship, however, and have introduced a person to Christ, they might be more receptive to a conversation about how their actions are bringing harm. May God grant us clarity and discernment to affirm and challenge in the ways that are most helpful for the salvation of souls.

Questions to Bring to Prayer

1. In the beginning of this chapter, we talked about goodness as being like the grapefruit of the fruits of the Spirit. What habits or behaviors have you struggled to implement in the past because you thought they were good, even if not immediately pleasing? Do you still struggle to implement them? Why or why not?

2. What will you want to be able to reflect back on as your legacy, the signs that you lived a good life? Whatever stage of life you are in now, do you feel you are building toward that legacy?

3. One of the best ways to call forth the potential for goodness within others is to catch them doing the right thing. What person in your life right now would be most blessed if you were more intentional about affirming them when you catch them doing the right thing?

Dear Heavenly Father, you are so good. We thank you for pouring out your goodness upon us and also for filling us with the fruit of your goodness so that we might grow in likeness to you. Please Lord, help us magnify your glory to a world in need. This we pray for the salvation of souls and the glory of the kingdom, in your Spirit, through Jesus Christ. Amen.

CHAPTER 9

Faithfulness

Well done, my good and faithful servant. Since you were faithful in small matters, I will give you great responsibilities. Come, share your master's joy. (Matthew 25:21)

It is a comfort to know that we serve a God who is always faithful. In fact, the entire Old Testament could be summed up as a collection of covenants between God and his people. A covenant is far more intense and binding than a contract. A contract is a legal agreement between parties stipulating that if you do A, I will do B. Should you in the future fail to deliver on the promise of A, I am no longer bound to fulfill the promise of B. A covenant is a binding agreement that stipulates that I will hold up my end even if you should fail to hold up yours.

A covenant would not make sense for an exchange of goods or services. For that, a contract works really well. Covenants are for more intimate exchanges, such as in marriage. A couple promise to love one another, honor one another, serve one another, and be faithful to one another, regardless of the circumstances. Even if you sometimes fail me, I will not let myself off the hook but will continue to do my best to not fail you. Throughout the Old Testament, God remains faithful to his covenant promises despite his people often failing to hold up their end of the bargain.

Of course we want to develop the fruit of faithfulness as it relates to our relationship with God. We want to hold up our commitment to grow as his disciples, to pray daily, to serve those whom God places in our care, and to avoid the sins that separate us from him. These things go without saying, but God wants even more from us.

I think he wants us to be faithful to the people in our lives. If Christians are going to astound those around us through the fruit of faithfulness, then we need to become staggeringly faithful friends. This goes especially for those who do not return the favor. Many people far from God today may be used to being regularly disappointed by the people in their lives. What if we could surprise and delight them by being faithful, especially when they don't expect it?

What Is Faithfulness, Really?

Common to any notion of faithfulness is an intentional perseverance on behalf of another. There are several characteristics specific to this fruit that we can model as God brings it to full growth in our lives. Here are just a few examples of what faithfulness can encompass.

Be a Woman or Man of Your Word

Jesus tells us in the Gospel of Matthew to "Let your 'Yes' mean 'Yes,' and your 'No' mean 'No'" (Matthew 5:37). Do you know someone who makes clear decisions and then always follows through on what they promise? It can be so refreshing to lean on their faithfulness. Conversely, when someone has a regular habit of failing to follow through on their promises, interactions with them can be exhausting.

I recently connected with a friend who works in young adult ministry. She said that it has become common for young people she works with to avoid breaking promises by simply hedging their bets. When asked if they want to come to a party on Friday night, for example, they say, "Yeah, I might stop by" or "Sure, if I have enough time, I'll come for a while." Though it may sound great that they are not breaking promises, it's not so great that they are failing to even make promises. There is no faithfulness at work here. True faithfulness must be decisive!

We are sons and daughters of God. When God speaks, his word does not return to him empty (see Isaiah 55:11). As his offspring in Christ Jesus, we should not be flippant about what we promise, but we *should* make promises. They need not always be profound or deep. Even small commitments are a way to model the fruit of faithfulness, grow in it, and give glory to God.

Fulfill Life Promises

Over the last several decades, we have been struggling with the reality of a priest shortage in the Catholic Church in the United States. Fewer men are choosing to pour themselves out in the great gift of love that is the priesthood. At face value, we could just write this off with the excuse that too much is being expected of them. There is certainly some truth to that, but it's only half of the story. Similarly, fewer men and women are choosing to pour themselves out to each other through marriage.

God has created each of us to fulfill a role in life that is specific to us, to make a gift of ourselves to others. For some, it might be a call to marriage. Others might be called to stay single but to serve in some other way. Single people often have the freedom and mobility to give of themselves in heroic ways that are closed to married people.

Of course, no one should ever rush into the decision to promise themselves to one call or another. Discernment is essential. People should take whatever time they need to carefully listen to the voice of God before making any commitment. In the case of our own children, Hollie and I taught them to pray that God would reveal his plan to them—we started doing this well before they could understand what the concept meant. We hope that as they continue to mature, God will make his call crystal clear in their lives.

Once we discover our call, we should commit ourselves without reserve and then remain faithful to it without fail.

Faithful to People

There is another, deeper level of faithfulness. We can be faithful to specific people, believing in them even when they do not believe in themselves. We can make ourselves available to encourage them, cry with them, or even pray with them. We can be a rock in their lives. We can see them as their best possible selves, even in moments when they are showing the rest of the world their worst. When other people give up on them, we can remain faithful. Even when they have betrayed or abandoned us in the past, by the power of Christ, we can be the source of light that they need.

Sharing Our Faith through Faithfulness

Truly faithful friends do not attach strings, especially strings of conversion. We touched on this a bit in the chapter on love, but it applies here as well. To truly be a faithful friend means staying beside the people in our lives, even if they never come to faith, even if they once had faith in Jesus, but then lost it. Otherwise, we would not be offering true friendship; we'd be using them to achieve a goal of our own.

This can be a difficult concept for us to wrap our minds around. How do we practice authentically faithful friendship with someone who is far from God? How do we go on longing for them to come to conversion while also overcoming the temptation to attach strings of conversion to our friendship? After all, a Christian should never say with their words or actions, "I will be your friend if you start coming to church and following Jesus."

Every analogy breaks down, but I'd like to use one to try to clarify this idea. Picture something you love doing that has transformed your life, something you would love to share with others. I'm talking about the kind of activity that has enhanced your life and made you more richly yourself than you knew you could be. I have heard some people describe joining a CrossFit gym in this way. For others, it might be learning to play chess or participating in musical theater.

For me, it was taking a speech class back in ninth grade. Before that class, I was afraid of my own shadow. I felt that every time I tried to talk to people, they knew I wasn't good enough. Why were they wasting their time on me? Then, in this speech class, I learned how to communicate with grace and composure. I learned how to carry myself with my shoulders back and a spring in my step. I learned how to believe in myself and that I actually had things worth sharing.

I ended up joining the speech and debate team and stuck with it through all four years of high school. No longer was I constantly anxious or timid. Okay, I was probably still pretty awkward, but not quite as awkward as I had been before speech.

As you might expect, I knew the positive impact this activity had had on me, so I was excited to share it with other people. I invited almost anyone I interacted with regularly to join the speech and debate team. Some I worked on for years, trying to convince them, but I never refused to associate with someone who wasn't interested. We stayed friends. I might have periodically revisited invitations to the team, but I never once distanced myself from someone just because they didn't share my commitment to a life-changing hobby. If I had, you would rightly call me shallow.

As much as I valued the impact of speech on my own life, it is immeasurably insignificant compared to the transformational potential and eternal ramifications of a life of grace. Yet I think the comparison remains valid. A faithful friend remains faithful regardless of whether or not we see a desired change, even a change as important as coming to the gospel.

A Key for Faithfulness

Rooting out distractions will help us unlock growth in faithfulness. Faithful students put their television at the other end of the house so that they can overcome the temptation to binge on Netflix instead of studying. Faithful spouses avoid circumstances such as being alone with another person in a compromising situation, especially if alcohol is involved. Distractions lower our resistance and lead us to act in ways we might not even want to act. The distractions of social media or mindless gaming are especially tempting today. If we are too busy with them, we won't be available either to God or to the people in our lives. Even good hobbies can be distracting if we find we are dedicating too much time to them. We only have so many hours in a day.

Here's a great way to check how much time you devote to distractions: keep a record of how you spend your time over the course of one week. How much time do you dedicate to prayer, to work, to other people, to rest? How much time do you spend on hobbies? How much on activities that are nothing more than a waste of your potential? If you finish a week of such assessment and find you are happy with how you spent the time, then you are probably doing okay on the distractions front. If, instead, you see that you need to revise your days in order to reduce distractions, you are free to do so in the next week and the next, perhaps keeping track of the time until you are sure you have a better handle on distractions.

This may take a lot of work in the short term, but the benefits are worth it. First, you can discover where your hours are going and then eliminate or reduce those distractions that are stealing your potential for fruit. Second, you may find that you are actually using your time more productively than you thought. You may find a few areas to improve, but you can also stop giving yourself a hard time for the things you don't get done! Someone who has taken the time to root out distractions and busyness is simply freer to develop the fruit of faithfulness.

A Challenge of Faithful Prayer

I want to also offer a challenge based on the suggestion of my friend, Kevin Cotter, who works for an organization called Amazing Parish. Take out a piece of paper and write down the names of five people for whom you will pray every day so that they might come to know the love of Jesus Christ. Pray also that the Holy Spirit might bring about appropriate moments for you to witness to them—circumstances in which you can naturally and appropriately share your faith.

The first name on your list should be the person you are closest to, or the person you think is closest to coming to the gospel. The fifth should be someone you are also close to, though not as close to as the first—essentially, all the names should be of people with whom you have a real relationship. Over weeks, months, or even years, the order of the people on the list might change. In fact, some people might even fall off the list. Either way, commit now that you will faithfully pray for these people every day. You might never know, on this side of eternity, the power of such intercession, but commit yourself now to be *faithful* in your prayers on their behalf.

Questions to Bring to Prayer

1. Earlier in this chapter, we explored three different examples of faithfulness. Has one of these been easy for you? Hard for you? Can you think of any additional examples?

2. Whom do you know, personally, who has exhibited faithful friendship toward another, even when the other person has not returned the same level of commitment? What have you learned from their example?

3. On a scale of one to ten, how well do you think you have rooted out unhelpful distractions from your life? What is one thing you can do to start moving the number up the scale next week?

Dear Heavenly Father, please develop within us the fruit of faithfulness. May we be faithful as you are faithful, as your saints and servants throughout history have been faithful. May we become people who give our word and keep it, in small things and in large. May we be faithful and prayerful friends for all those whom you are inviting us to love. For the salvation of souls and the glory of the kingdom, through the Spirit, in Jesus' name. Amen.

CHAPTER 10

Gentleness

Let your speech always be gracious, seasoned with salt, so that you know how you should respond to each one. (Colossians 4:6)

When she was four years old, my daughter Lillie demonstrated to me some of her unique capacity for gentleness—she is tenderhearted and deeply concerned about the well-being of others. I discovered this while trying (and I emphasize trying) to play my guitar. I don't have a lot of aptitude for musical instruments, but twice a year, around Christmas and St. Patrick's Day, I like to pull out my old guitar and hack my way through a few festive songs.

One evening in December, Lillie plopped down to be my audience through what was probably an award-worthy worst version ever of "Please Come Home for Christmas." It's about a guy who is hoping his love will return to him for the holiday season, and it has a fun, soulful quality to it.

As I strummed the last couple of chords, I expected to look up and see my daughter smiling and swaying along. Instead, I was shocked to discover that she was bawling her eyes out! These weren't just tears but the heaving gasps of someone who is in full-on crying mode. I thought, *Please tell me it wasn't that bad.* When I asked her why she was crying, she said, "Oh,

Daddy! It is so *sad*! He doesn't have his love." I couldn't help chuckling as I held her and tried to comfort her. Even though it was funny and a little sad, I pray to God that she please never lose such sweetness.

What Is Gentleness, Really?

Kindness and gentleness are so closely related that it can be difficult to differentiate them. For the purpose of this book, the chapter on kindness focused on our actions and the impact they have. In this chapter, I instead want to focus on how to perform our actions in a Christlike way. Growing in this fruit of the Holy Spirit should make a difference not only in what we do but in how we do it.

The gentleness with which we act toward others should confirm that we have their best interests in mind. For example, there is no way to gently cut someone off in traffic. We sometimes associate gentleness with a soft or quiet voice, but that is not enough to be a true marker of the fruit. After all, if you are lying about someone or trashing their reputation, it doesn't matter how softly you speak. Your actions are not expressing the spiritual fruit of gentleness.

Doing things with warmth captures something of the concept of gentleness. Think of a time when someone greeted you warmly. They were attentive and gracious, and they conveyed that they were truly happy to see you. If you can really remember such a time, I bet that even the memory of it makes you feel warmer inside.

From the earliest days of the Church, Christians have performed what we know as the corporal and spiritual works of mercy. The corporal, or bodily, works of mercy include feeding the hungry, giving drink to the thirsty, clothing the naked, sheltering the homeless, visiting the sick, visiting the imprisoned, and burying the dead. The spiritual works of mercy include counseling the doubtful, instructing the ignorant, admonishing the sinner, comforting the sorrowful, forgiving injuries, bearing wrongs, and praying for others. Now try to picture anyone performing one of these acts without warmth. Probably not a good idea, right? Admonishing a sinner without warmth? Yeah, that one is not going to go so well. The more we can marry our acts of kindness with a disposition of gentleness, the more authentically we can testify to the glory of God by our lives.

This gentleness makes us more effective in our life calling as well. Teachers and parents will be far more effective if they can be gentle. I would much rather be cared for by a medical professional whose bedside manner reflects this fruit. And a spirit of gentleness is absolutely critical for those caring for anyone coming out of an abusive situation or an emotional crisis.

Battles All around Us

It's not easy to maintain a spirit of gentleness, especially in the face of division. If you want to see this at its most comic, attend a kids' soccer game some Saturday morning. Make sure you don't know anyone on either team. That way, you won't be emotionally invested, and you can simply observe.

Inevitably, during the game, the referee will have to make a difficult call. Every spectator wearing a red shirt will erupt in raucous disapproval. "How could he miss that?!" they will shout. "Is he *blind* or something?" Everyone wearing a blue shirt will insist that the referee absolutely got the call right. Both sides will leave wholly convinced and defensive about the fact that they are right and that everyone who disagrees with them is inexcusably wrong.

It's no better at the level of professional sports. Even with fifteen cameras covering the action and the availability of slow-motion replays, people are far more likely to see the data in a way that supports their team rather than their opponents.

And these examples are just from sports! Imagine how serious this divisive atmosphere can be when it comes to things that actually matter, such as our jobs, our communities, or the social issues that affect us all. I'm not suggesting that truth is a matter of one's perspective. Far from it! I simply want to demonstrate that it's easy to become emotionally invested in a position that might be false and might lead to really unhealthy conflict. To navigate such an environment and advocate for truth and goodness, we Christians must become people of great gentleness.

The Blame Game

Jesus warns us that "no town or house divided against itself will stand" (Matthew 12:25). I'm sure that this will not come as a shock to anyone, but sometimes even people in the Church can be divisive. Not every church office is a place of deep harmony and mutual respect. Having worked in apostolates, parishes, and at the diocesan level, I have had the opportunity to see heroic examples of the fruits of the Spirit at work in some staff members. However, I have also seen people be cruel and deeply negative toward each other. I have seen gossip, suspicion, and especially blame work their way into the culture of Christian organizations.

Parish leaders have blamed diocesan leaders when things go wrong. Diocesan leaders have blamed parish leaders. Catechists have blamed parents, and parents blame catechists. "If this person, or that person would just do things the way they are supposed to, everything would turn out great!" There is always someone else we could blame for things not going the way we want. I admit that in my worst moments, I too have participated in the blame game at times. God, forgive me.

It can feel so good to blame someone else when things are not going the way we would like. It can even be addictive. We get this little rush of righteousness at the idea that we have it all figured out. We get a sense of belonging, as if we are on the inside of the elite group of people who really understand things. Best of all, if it's someone else's fault, then we don't have to change anything about our actions or behavior. It's not our responsibility.

Fortunately, taking the opposite tack can also be extremely energizing. When we make a commitment to quit wasting time complaining about what we cannot control, we liberate ourselves—our gifts and abilities—for maximum impact. It might feel good to say "This is their fault." But it always feels better to say "I take responsibility for the future."

Transition from Nice to Gentle

My wife grew up in the great state of Minnesota where being nice to others is so firmly ingrained in the culture that they even have a name for it: Minnesota Nice. It's wonderful, when visiting, to experience what life can be like when people embrace a social expectation of politeness and respect toward others. Yet the cultural norm of niceness is not always synonymous with the spiritual fruit of gentleness. If we want to truly model our faith in a way that astounds others, we need to move past the natural human level of niceness to the authentic superhuman level of gentleness. As we strive to open ourselves up to this spiritual fruit, here are a few distinctions to keep in mind.

Distinction 1: Self-Interest vs. Others-Interest

We might choose to act *nicely* out of self-interest. Spiritual gentleness always flows from a desire for the well-being of others. Nice people can act the way they do for a host of reasons. They might simply be doing what is socially expected. They might be trying to avoid the consequences of conflict. Maybe they want to make a good impression in order to get something they want. I once heard a waiter jokingly say that the person he is when he is waiting tables is completely different from the person he is the rest of the time. What's going on there? Most likely he is pretending to be nice because he knows that's the best way to get a good tip.

As we grow in true gentleness, our motivations simplify as well. We begin to act with warmth and friendliness because we genuinely enjoy treating people well. If we happen to be waiters, I suspect that, over time, we actually get better tips than the waitstaff who are faking it. True gentleness of heart warms those who experience it.

Distinction 2: Deception vs. Truth

We might act *nicely* out of a failure to commit to the truth. We act gently only when we are deeply committed to sharing the truth, though in the most caring way possible. We all make wrong decisions from time to time. It might be over something inconsequential, such as which way is the fastest way to get to work, or it might be over something really important, such as choices that damage our most significant relationships.

Nice people, as well as gentle people, hold their tongue over something trivial. When it comes to something serious, however, the person who is only nice treats the damaging issue exactly as they would treat the unimportant issue. "Why upset the applecart? It doesn't affect me." As we become gentle, however, we are willing to speak up to deliver an uncomfortable message. Of course, even in the midst of doing so, we ought to never lose sight of gentleness. We should pick the right times and circumstances. We should consider admitting some past error of our own if we discern that doing so will make it easier for the chided person to save face.

Of course, we can take this willingness to speak up too far as well. If we are always willing to deliver a hard truth, we might not be more authentic than the nice person; we might just be a busybody. In every circumstance, we must take great care and use discernment in order to choose the gentle and appropriate response.

Distinction 3: Turmoil vs. Peace

Acting nicely can cover up the fact that we operate from a place of inner turmoil. The gentle person operates from a place of deep peace. If our niceness is a mere façade, it can conceal a less-than-loving attitude toward the person with whom we are speaking. When this is the case, our niceness allows a kind of cease-fire to take root inside us. Should we say what we really think to this person, or should we keep it together? We might project a peaceful demeanor but be wrestling with inner turmoil.

Conversely, as we grow into true gentleness, a deep river of peace flows forth from within as a gift of God. Even when facing difficult situations and people, we possess a sense of inner consolation from which we draw strength. We also can see the inherent goodness even of those people we find most challenging. In gentleness, we patiently love them for who God has created them to be.

Distinction 4: Exhausted vs. Energized

Operating on the natural level of niceness can be exhausting. Operating on the supernatural level of gentleness, however, is energizing. It's too hard to fake being nice over the long haul—cracks will show. Exhaustion sets in until our efforts break down and until the not-so-nice self finally surfaces.

As we transition to gentleness, this vicious cycle becomes a virtuous cycle. The more we practice this fruit of the Spirit, the more it becomes second nature—easy and energizing. Authenticity reinforces healthy relationships. We come to perceive otherwise difficult circumstances and people no longer as burdens but as opportunities. The chance to practice our gentleness may even help us feel we are getting more out of life.

A Key to Gentleness

I wrestled long and hard with a key to gentleness and finally settled on simply slowing down as the best way to foster this gift within us. When I was about eight years old, my father took me out to our backyard to teach me how to catch a football. He would demonstrate patterns for me to run as if I were in a real game, and then he would toss me the ball. At first, I was too anxious and hurried. I would reach out toward the ball and slap my hands together to try to catch it. Inevitably, it would just bounce away from me.

After several rounds of this, we took a break. My father then gave me the hint that made all the difference. "Don't slap at the ball, but slow down and let it come to you," he said. "Pretend that it is a loaf of bread. If you try to smash it together, you will flatten the loaf. If you instead slow everything down and let it come to you, you can gently cradle the ball in your hands." Immediately, my completion percentage went up about 300 percent!

Hollie and I have learned that in our home, a sense of urgency is the number one action that leads to a lack of gentleness. Gentleness falls by the wayside when we operate from a ragged sense that whatever the problem or issue at hand, we must deal with it as quickly as possible. To combat such a reaction, all of us in the family take a time-out to catch our breath, reassess, and consider a more appropriate response. Even as my children approach their teenage years, when that panicky sense of urgency hits, we direct them to go to their rooms and count slowly to twenty. Making a deliberate attempt to slow down will almost always help anyone cope with even a momentary frustration. I cannot count all the times I have heard people say something they regretted because they didn't pause first.

Similarly, I always know I'll have a better day if I can start it with thirty to sixty minutes of quiet prayer and reflection. By slowing down my morning, I'm better prepared to face each opportunity and obstacle with a gentle hand.

Sharing Faith through Gentleness

As you wrestle with these concepts, do not beat yourself up if you keep falling back on the less-than-ideal experience of niceness. You are not alone. Gentleness develops within us only gradually, through grace, before it becomes a blessing to those around us, even if they don't recognize it as such. Gentleness does have the capacity to astound, but maybe not as often as other fruits, such as joy. True gentleness is so quiet and unassuming that it doesn't draw attention to itself and is easily overlooked.

Forgive me if I use a second football analogy in a chapter on gentleness, of all things! I once heard a commentator say that the center position on a football team is the least appreciated position of all. No one ever notices what the center does unless he does it wrong. In the same way, very few people may notice if you have the fruit of gentleness, but many will likely notice if you don't. Maybe every once in a while, someone will be in a situation in which they really need your gentleness and will be grateful for it. Your gentleness really can smooth out human interactions, overcome conflict, and become an aid for others encountering God.

Questions to Bring to Prayer

1. How might the people in your home, church, and community uniquely and specifically benefit from your growing in gentleness?

2. In this chapter, we explored four distinctions between the natural strength of niceness and the supernatural fruit of gentleness. Which of these distinctions have you experienced in yourself or in others? What difference has the niceness or gentleness of another person made in your life?

3. We also explored examples of benefits that come from slowing down and not allowing urgency to lead you to act in a way that is ungentle. What habits can help you slow down?

Dear Heavenly Father, let us never be satisfied with the false fruit of niceness. In this world that is so often angry and divisive, give us, as your servants, the capacity to be a healing balm for others through the fruit of gentleness. This we ask for the salvation of souls and the glory of your kingdom, in Jesus, through his Holy Spirit. Amen!

CHAPTER 11

Self-Control

Therefore, let us not sleep as the rest do, but let us stay alert and sober. (1 Thessalonians 5:6)

Can I just say that when it comes to the *theory* of the fruits of the Spirit, I am *so* holy. It is only when I actually have to live them out that I find myself struggling. Theory is a piece of cake. It's in the daily practice, while living among real people who are testing my limits, that I fall down. St. Paul said much the same thing in his Letter to the Romans: "What I do, I do not understand. For I do not do what I want, but I do what I hate" (Romans 7:15). If you are like St. Paul and me, struggling to do the good you want to do, then maybe you too are ready to ask God to grow within you the fruit of self-control.

When I first started to pray that God would help me develop this fruit, I thought my progress would come about primarily through an act of the will. If I clenched my teeth and tried really hard, I could get things right. None of the fruits develop this way, as we have seen, but we might be tempted to think that self-control is an exception to the rule. It is not. We grow in self-control, not by tightening up every muscle in our bodies, but, rather, by releasing our tension and cooperating with God's gentle guidance. This fruit is not marked by intensity but by serenity and composure.

What Is Self-Control, Really?

The fruit of self-control involves far more than not losing our temper. Any time we know the right course of action but allow our feelings to lead us in another direction, we experience a lapse in self-control. Any time we listen, instead, to our conscience, we experience a victory in self-control. Does this mean that all excitement or emotion is wrong? Far from it!

God made us with the ability and the instinct to relish moments of rapture and enthusiasm. The last time you cheered your favorite sports team or shouted in excitement when your daughter was accepted into college, God cheered with you. This capacity we have to be swept up and fully embrace the moment is a genuine good. Maybe many of you have even had such moments in your prayer before God.

Self-control, however, asks an important question: "How far will my enthusiasm take me?" When I am cheering and screaming alongside forty-seven thousand other fans at a football game, I haven't lost control of myself. My excitement is self-controlled, and I should be able to turn it on or off without too much difficulty. This is the opposite of the loss of control that happens when mob mentality takes over in a group. Otherwise sane and stable people give themselves up to the moment, and when things go too far, they can't deescalate their emotions. How far have they let their enthusiasm take them? Much too far.

I hope none of us ever have to fight off the lure of a mob mentality, but we can all get carried away during other moments in life. Too much of a good thing is not a good thing.

One piece of cake was fantastic, but that second didn't feel quite right . . . and that third one, well, that was definitely not living up to my full dignity as a child of God.

This is especially the case when it comes to a drug like alcohol, for example. Beer, wine, and spirits may feel good because they have the ability to help us relax, but they also weaken our ability to manage our actions. For some people, even one drink is one too many. Getting drunk is never a good idea because it is the very picture of a loss of control. Just as one's muscles become less responsive, so does one's decision-making prowess. When we drink to excess, we inevitably take things too far. We cease to be who we really are.

This is not to say that disciples should fail to enjoy life. Christ came to bring us abundant life, even in our lives here on earth. Some people think of Christians as spoilsports because they exercise self-control. To be fair, some of us Christians actually are spoilsports, so critics do have a point. It can be tempting to look at the dangers of losing control and conclude that we are better off not showing emotion at all. That's not living. That's hiding from life. Self-control means God leads us to that perfect balance of relishing life, with all its joys and challenges, without losing ourselves or ignoring the needs of others.

Sharing Faith through Self-Control

When self-control is at work in our lives, I think that the impact on the people around us is similar to the impact of the fruit of peace. People who operate from a position of self-control are comfortable in their own skin. This enables the people around them to feel at ease, as well. Further, self-control frees people to face situations of trial and adversity with grace. They don't ever have to live in dread. Like the faithful person, they are reliable even in the heat of the moment.

Of course, facing difficult circumstances is not the same thing as seeking them. Someone filled with this fruit does not necessarily jump out of a perfectly good plane just for the fun of it. They would, however, have no qualms about jumping if the situation required it. They are brave, but they are not brash. So too, when it comes to sharing the faith, they are bold but not foolish. They know when to speak and when to keep silent. They are attuned to the Spirit. They are joyful, but their joy is self-controlled, not likely to be off-putting. They are peaceful, but their peace isn't an excuse for passivity. Self-control works with all the fruits of the Spirit, in a way, so as to polish those fruits.

Ultimately, if love is the cornerstone of all the fruits, then I think it's fair to say that self-control is their capstone—the peak, the fruit of the Spirit that brings the other fruits into full alignment.

A Key to Self-Control

Just as a key to the fruit of love is spending time with God, so a key to self-control is developing a hunger to honor God in all our thoughts, words, and actions. In this regard, no reflection on this topic would be complete without at least briefly considering that famous moment in the temple when Jesus displayed such anger: "He overturned the tables of the money changers and the seats of those who were selling doves. He did not permit anyone to carry anything through the temple area" (Mark 11:15-16). In light of this Scripture passage, a friend of mine once joked that the next time people tell him to act more Christlike, he is going to remind them that, technically, flipping over tables remains an option!

But what is going on here? Jesus, who seems so gentle and patient throughout the Scriptures, has a moment of intense zeal that leaves many of us, Christians and non-Christians alike, scratching our heads. If we truly believe that Jesus is the sinless Son of God, then we cannot simply dismiss this as a lapse in judgment. Though it might not be immediately apparent, his actions were more than just excusable. They were justified. In short, he did the right thing. Rather than suffer a loss of self-control, he was appropriately managing his emotions.

How can that be?

I will not claim to understand this question exhaustively, but I think it is helpful to look at the question in light of this key to self-control, honoring God. Jesus was exercising self-control even in the temple by honoring God through his actions. First, he does so by honoring his Father's mission to reconcile the world. Notice how Jesus only speaks harshly in moments where people need to be convicted of their sin. He doesn't condemn the woman caught in adultery because she already knows she needs to repent. He does condemn the Pharisees, on the other hand, because they aren't even aware of their need to repent, much less how their behavior negatively impacts others.

Also, notice how Jesus does not speak in anger so as to defend his own honor, but, rather, that of the Father. If we ever feel tempted to indulge in a moment of self-righteous indignation, it is important that we catch ourselves and ask if what we do is really for God or for our own sake. Are we moving forward God's kingdom, or are we simply defending ourselves?

Far from defending himself, Jesus' display of emotion in the temple actually sets up the profundity of his own upcoming sacrifice on the cross. He declares the need to purify the earthly temple, and then he makes the ultimate act of honor to the Father by laying down the temple of his own body for the forgiveness of sins, for the forgiveness even of those who violated the earthly temple.

May we too hunger to honor God by our thoughts, words, and actions. If we are wondering if something we might do or say would reflect a loss of self-control, we can always ask ourselves, "Would this truly honor God?" The more we grow in all the fruits of the Spirit and the more we top off all the fruits with a measure of self-control, the more likely we are to answer that question rightly.

Questions to Bring to Prayer

1. Have you traditionally thought of self-control more as an act of hand-clenching willpower or more as a releasing to the grace of God? What difference does this make when it comes to facing difficult situations?

2. How do you think the ordinary people visiting the temple that day experienced the moment when Jesus drove out the money changers and flipped over the tables? Can you imagine yourself in that scene? How would his actions have encouraged you to rethink how you honor God in your life?

3. What action or change can you make today to more fully allow God to grow the fruit of self-control in your life? Have you called on the Holy Spirit for the grace to meet your need?

Dear Heavenly Father, we thank you for filling us with the grace we need to receive the spiritual fruit of self-control. As we face the trials and the temptations of this life, may we never lose sight of our call to glorify you. By the sacrifice of your Son, Jesus, nurture each fruit within us for the salvation of souls and the glory of the kingdom, with the Spirit, in Jesus' name. Amen.

CHAPTER 12

But How Do We Do It?

He said to them, "Go into the whole world and proclaim the gospel to every creature." (Mark 16:15)

Okay! We've made it through reflections on all nine of the fruits of the Spirit. I hope some new insights have emerged to challenge you to grow in service to God and his people. I'd like to conclude this book with a few thoughts that bring us back to our starting point: will growing in the fruits of the Spirit really help us share our faith with others? After all, we could just focus on our own personal growth and edification rather than on sharing the gospel. As we have seen, however, the fruits of the Spirit ought to not only bring us closer to God but also closer to other people, hopefully drawing them to the unfailing light of the Father. Now that we have an idea of what it might be like for us to experience the transformation that comes from growing in the fruits, let's reconsider what it means to evangelize.

Not a Computation

A good friend of mine, Peter Andrastek, works for a great ministry called The Evangelical Catholic. He and his team assist churches in releasing the missionary capacity of their congregants by discipling people in the context of small groups. A key part of their effort is not just the discipling of current Christians but also intentionally reaching out to those who do not yet know Jesus. Once, while he was giving a presentation, someone asked him, "What words should we say to someone to get them to want to explore who Jesus is?"

Peter responded, "Well, it depends on the unique circumstances of the person, how you know them, and the nature of your relationship with them."

The questioner then turned again to Peter with a sheepish grin and said, "Yeah, but what do we say?"

I think we all face the danger of treating people as if they were a computation for which we need to calculate an answer. We think if we can just input the right words into their system, they will have the response we want and come to conversion. I guess it is not surprising that we sometimes feel this way. After all, when programmers put the right formula into their computers, the computers provide the exact responses they're seeking.

Similarly, even God allows us to receive grace through specific formulas. The key to accessing baptismal grace is sprinkling or immersion, accompanied by the words, "I baptize you in the name of the Father, and of the Son, and of the Holy Spirit." Likewise, the teaching tradition of Jesus and the apostles has been handed down for two millennia by means of creeds that are a kind of formula. It is no wonder we have such a propensity to take a formulaic approach to evangelizing.

Not Answers but Questions

One of the best lessons I have learned working with Alpha is the value of asking questions. Before Alpha, I prided myself on my capacity to provide comprehensive and thorough answers to the questions of faith people brought me. They might ask me a simple question, such as whether Jesus is God or man. I would then pull out my fire hose and drench them with every bit of information I knew on the topic. I would give them dates, events, and even the names of saints involved in the process of clarifying this question. I failed to realize that they would often leave the conversation more confused than when they arrived.

Today, I am far more concerned with trying to understand why the person is asking the questions they are asking. What is going on in their heart? I am reminded that Jesus in the Scriptures asked hundreds of questions, but he only answered other people's questions a handful of times. By asking questions and giving people the space to share what they think, we are actually inviting them to process and discover for themselves what they believe. If we are praying in the midst of this, we can be assured that the Holy Spirit will also be guiding them toward all truth in the midst of conversations.

There is certainly a place for sharing facts and explanations about the faith. Catechesis of already committed disciples is especially concerned with this, but even those who are unevangelized need someone providing accessible answers to their questions at times. That being said, our beginning point with most people today has to be asking questions that lead them into a quest for answers.

Knowing and Sharing Your Story

If we are people living as disciples of Jesus Christ, month after month and year after year, we ought to be developing scores of stories about the ways God is moving us. Each new season should have some lesson we have learned, sin we have repented of, or way in which God has used us to serve the kingdom. When I was a teenager, we made a big deal at church of having everyone write down their witness—how they came to believe in God and the truths of the Church. Sometimes, we would create a platform for people to get up and recite their witness before an audience. While this might be a great way to reinforce what God is doing for us, I don't think it helps prepare us very well to share with others.

Effective witness to another person almost never happens as a monologue. It is a conversation in which we briefly and naturally share our experience. Ideally, we should be able to tailor what we share based on the specific conversation we are having. Now, there will be a temptation to overly manage this tailoring in a computational way, again treating people like a program. Instead, just try to relax and enjoy the conversation with your friend. Here is an example that might be helpful.

Brandon Sanderson Fandom

I am a huge fan of an author named Brandon Sanderson. I first came across his books about three years ago, and I was blown away by his story-telling ability. I have since read just about everything he has ever written. Not only do I love reading his books for myself, but I have also become somewhat of an apostle for his work, sharing his books with several other people in my life. Based on my experience with each specific person, I can share what I think they will most appreciate about his books. To one I might say, "I love the way he tells a compelling story without needing to add a bunch of R-rated content. It's all pretty clean." To another I might say, "The situational humor he builds in is absolutely brilliant, and it will keep you laughing hours after reading it." To a third, I might emphasize how impressive I find his action scenes or his creative building of distinct cultures.

These appeals are not carefully reasoned computations. They are simple observations based on our shared points of interest or concern. I know the other person will value them as well because we are in relationship with each other. I have first listened and gotten to really know the person with whom I am sharing. Therefore, I have a pretty good sense regarding what they will or will not appreciate.

In the same way, God will open very different doors to discovering the gospel for the people with whom we interact. Jesus revealed to us that he is "the way and the truth and the life" (John 14:6). Maybe some people need to first discover him as the Way, the pathway to a meaningful life. Others need to first be convinced that he is the Truth, that the revelations of Scripture stand up to logical scrutiny. Still others need healing from Jesus, that they might encounter him first as the Life. Ultimately, we want them to discover him as all three, but the more we can tailor our initial sharing to their particular needs, the better we can serve them.

Simple but Not Easy

What I am describing here is not a quick-fix solution to evangelization. No, this is all about developing ongoing loving relationships with people. In the midst of those relationships, we really take the time to get to know them. Then, we propose some element of the gospel to them and invite them to explore further. That invite might even be to come to an Alpha, or it might just be to have another conversation with us. Sometimes, people will accept our invitations, and sometimes they will not. If we are truly modeling the fruits of the Spirit, we will have more opportunities to make still more invites in the future.

Pray, Pray, Pray

How do we do it? How do we actually save people and destine them for an eternity of intimate connection with Jesus? This is so simple! *We don't.* I will never save anyone. You will never save anyone. The resource of Alpha has never saved anyone. The only thing we can do is accept our call to participate in what the Holy Spirit is already doing.

In the beginning of this book, I warned about the dangers of relying too heavily on experts, explanations, and events. No combination of strategic factors will ultimately be successful in leading people to encounter the deep, abiding joy of the Christian life. Only God can do that. So everything we do should not revolve around our eloquence or our plans. It should revolve around our leaning into the presence of the Holy Spirit.

When I was a teenager, first learning about the Holy Spirit in preparation for Confirmation, I heard the Holy Spirit described as a dove, a flame, and as wind. Tragically, I don't really think it stuck with me at the time that he is so much more. The Holy Spirit is a *person*! He is here in our midst right now. Jesus Christ actually ascended to the Father specifically so that he could send us the Holy Spirit.

Do we really take Jesus at his word when he says, "It is better for you that I go" (John 16:7)? If so, then the Spirit is not just some ethereal essence watching from the clouds and rooting for us. He longs to be intimately involved in all we think, say, and do to the glory of God the Father. More than being someone available on our team, he is inviting us to be on *his* team. Every time we say, "Come, Holy Spirit," I believe we are improving the trajectory of the world. Let us never be fooled. It is only through prayer and the power of the Holy Spirit that the kingdom of God will grow. Daily intimacy with this third Person of the Trinity leads to cooperation, to evangelization, and hopefully to fruit.

As we conclude this reflection together, I would like to end by asking afresh for the guidance and direction of the Holy Spirit.

Come, Holy Spirit. Come, Holy Spirit. Come, Holy Spirit. We thank you for your presence in our Christian lives, and we set ourselves at your disposal. Please enrich us with gifts, insights, and fruit, that we might be rightly empowered to participate in your building up of the kingdom. Draw us toward those who are most desperately in need of the joy of the gospel, and align us with your plans to participate in effectively revealing life in Jesus to them. This we pray for the salvation of souls, to the glory of God the Father. Amen.

AFTERWORD

How This Book Came About

Thank you so much for going on this journey with me and exploring the fruits of the Spirit. It was a joy to write this book, and it continues to challenge me to better cooperate with grace in my own life. I hope you find it beneficial in your efforts to live and share the faith as well.

For those interested, I want to offer a few words about how this book came to be and the special role that Alpha has played in shaping my understanding of mission. I've spent the last several years serving as the national director for Alpha in a Catholic Context in the United States. This experience has led me to a growing conviction that we need to revolutionize nearly everything about how we prepare ourselves to evangelize—that is, to share the joy of the gospel with an unbelieving world.

I owe an immense debt of gratitude to Alpha and to its pioneers. The organization continues to be a place of ongoing growth for me. It has helped to shape my understanding of what it means to build God's kingdom. Best of all, it is a place where I am challenged and encouraged to meet Jesus daily. Any effort justly called evangelization is not primarily about theories or methods. It is not about psychology or clever arguments. It is an encounter with Jesus, who is not only alive but is the very gift of life himself.

Even as I write this, it's strange to speak about him in such an abstract way, as if he isn't here with me as I write, as if he isn't present to you while you read this. He came into the world not to condemn us, but that we might be saved through him. He even allows us simple, humble, broken men and women to participate in the building up of his kingdom here on earth. His Great Commission to the apostles still applies to each and every one of us today. You are commissioned to *go and make disciples of all nations that they might be baptized in the name of the Father, the Son, and the Holy Spirit, and taught to observe all he commanded* (see Matthew 28:19-20).

Before coming to Alpha, I had worked in parishes and in other apostolates. I had served in Christian radio and been involved in countless ministries. In each case, I was always left wondering whether or not the work I was doing would truly make a meaningful difference in the building of God's kingdom. Since the day I started working with Alpha, I have stopped wondering. I now get to see on a daily basis that God really is using us to change the world. I get to see the individual people whose lives are changed when they discover Christ. I get to visit with the priests and pastoral workers who have found a new purpose as they move from maintenance to mission. I simply cannot describe to you the privilege it is to contribute to such a movement!

This is not to discount the many ministries and individuals who work tirelessly in one area of the Church or another without seeing the fruits of their labors. As the Gospel reminds us, "One sows and another reaps" (John 4:37). I pray God will abundantly bless those who sacrifice for the kingdom despite not directly experiencing the results. When and where there is fruit, however, we all share in rejoicing over it.

As of this writing, well over twelve hundred Catholic parishes in the United States are actively running Alphas, leading about one hundred thousand people each year to the opportunity for a life-changing encounter with Jesus. These churches see people developing an intimate connection with God—both those who are already churchgoers and those with no previous faith background. These same guests then develop as leaders who invite still more people into the story. As exciting as this news is, let us not be fooled into thinking Alpha is a silver bullet. Sadly, some churches make the mistake of trying to take a shortcut with their Alpha initiative. They see that Alpha has developed an array of powerful videos, and they mistakenly conclude that it is the videos that do the evangelizing.

The truth is that while the content of the Alpha films is exceptional and their winsome style is ideal for starting a faith conversation, the videos are only one small piece of the greater success of Alpha. Many of us at Alpha even refer to the films as the smallest and least important piece of the process. Instead, the creation of a truly welcoming environment, the generous meal served at every meeting, the listening, and especially the prayer are the most profound elements of Alpha's success. I like to say that *Alpha is simply a platform we create. We focus on inviting our friends to show up, and we invite God to show up so they can meet each other.* When a church attempts to shortcut the environment and the larger experience of Alpha, very few guests will have sufficient opportunity to truly encounter the presence of God.

A second category of churches also ends up shortcutting the success of their Alphas. They do so by running it just for people *inside* their parish. When this happens, the church is often thrilled with the initial increase in passion among current churchgoers. The parish becomes friendlier and more connected. Then the parish leaders conclude that Alpha was a success, and they stop running it! In fact, Alpha had barely begun to accomplish what it can do.

While this tool is effective in serving parishioners, its true purpose as well as its best work is reaching those who are farthest from God. It is a means of casting out into the deep. Alpha can do its best work when used to help evangelize, to introduce people to Jesus. It provides a great opening for inviting your friends, neighbors, and loved ones who do not go to church to come and explore their questions. Alpha is especially able to reach those who are lost or broken, those on the spiritual margins—the very people who are most in need of the joy of the gospel.

Simple but Hard

Alpha is not a magic formula, nor is it just a collection of beautiful and compelling videos. As with so many things in life, what makes Alpha truly successful is simple and at the same time hard. We create a *simple* place where people and God can meet, and then we work really *hard* to make compelling invitations in order to bring people in.

It was this need to focus on invitation that convinced me to write about the fruits of the Spirit. I began to ask, "What if inviting people into an encounter with Jesus really is the most important thing we can ever do for them? What would that mean? How many more people could each of us invite? What do we need to change about our interactions with others? What do we need to change about ourselves?"

When I say we make compelling invitations to bring people in, I don't mean we make nice cards or advertisements. While there is nothing wrong with those, too often we fall for the illusion that a compelling marketing campaign can substitute for our becoming invitational people. We sanitize the hard work of connecting with broken people as if this were something that could ever be outsourced. Whether we use Alpha or some other tool or just focus on one-to-one evangelization, there is no shortcut for becoming an invitational people. To create marketing materials and call that invitation is as much a false shortcut as only showing the Alpha videos. In either case, we are skipping the messy and meaningful human interaction.

Are We Ready?

I once gave an Alpha training that went really well until the Q and A part of the session. At the back of the room was a pastor who was excited about inviting people to Alpha at his church. He started asking for insights about social media campaigns, posters, radio ads, and billboards. I told him those are all good things, but all they can do is normalize the idea of Alpha. "If you invite a friend to come check out Alpha, it is easier for him to say yes if he has heard of it somewhere before," I said. "It's great when your friend can say, 'Oh! I've heard of Alpha. Sure, I can come to an Alpha night.' Unfortunately, the vast majority of people who need Alpha will never come if the only invitation they experience is an ad."

When the pastor heard this, his excitement immediately diminished. Then he considered it further. I watched the look in his eyes shift from one of discouragement to one of outright worry or maybe even panic. He said to me, "Josh, you don't understand. The people in our church love each other so much that we don't even know any people who aren't Christians!"

Friends, here is a painful truth that took me far too long to learn. Unless the members of our communities are willing to build real relationships with those who are far from God, then they are not prepared to implement Alpha or any major effort of evangelization. It's intimidating to realize this, but we don't need to be afraid. We have a loving God who not only saves us but also equips us with every grace we could possibly need to do the work to which he is calling us. In fact, my goal in writing about the fruits of the Spirit is to familiarize us with some of the grace he is already providing.

Answering Common Questions

When I train a new parish for Alpha and help prepare the members to use its tools, their most common question is inevitably

"Is Alpha Catholic?" The answer is that Alpha is designed to be kerygmatic, which means it focuses on the basic elements of the faith that Catholics hold in common with all Christian believers. It is a methodology and a starting point, not a comprehensive catechesis. When this question comes up, I also share the testimonies of a great many high-profile Catholic leaders who testify to Alpha's authenticity and effectiveness in evangelizing both those in the pews and those outside the Church.

The second most common question people ask is, "What ought a church do immediately after Alpha?" I'm afraid there is no simple answer to this question. There are so many people with different backgrounds and spiritual needs who come through Alpha. Some are ready for Christian initiation. Others need more formation in prayer, the Bible, or the moral life. The one consistent need they all have is for an intimate Christian community that can both encourage and challenge them. For that reason, I always encourage parishes to begin building small Christian community groups as their immediate follow-up to Alpha. There, the community can discern together what each post-Alpha follower of Jesus might need.

The third most common question is this: "How do we get people to show up to Alpha to begin with?" I have wrestled with this question extensively and never been fully satisfied with what I am able to bring to the table. I guess you could say that this book is partially a deep pondering of that question. Whether we use Alpha or not, the question ultimately is, "How do we effectively introduce people to Jesus?"

If you do want to understand Alpha, I encourage you to begin by looking on our website—Alphausa.org—to find a training event. If you are looking for a book to teach you the ins and outs of achieving Alpha excellence, I cannot recommend any better option than Ron Huntley and Fr. James Mallon's book, *Unlocking Your Parish through Alpha.*

Regardless, if we are going to introduce an unbelieving world to the person of Jesus Christ, then we must bring so much more than strategy. We must *become* an invitational people. If you have the means, I encourage you to begin reflecting daily with a group of other Christians. Challenge each other to grow in faith each day. Encourage each other and pray for one another. Pray that God may "furnish you with all that is good, that you may do his will. May he carry out in you what is pleasing to him through Jesus Christ, to whom be glory forever [and ever]" (Hebrews 13:21).

The Fruits of the Spirit vs. the Seven Deadly Sins

As you move into the ongoing daily journey of allowing the fruit to develop, I have a little theory I want to share with you. If you find this to be helpful in your prayer and striving, then God be praised. If not, please feel free to disregard it.

I think there is a correlation between the nine fruits of the Spirit and what the Church has historically called the seven deadly sins. These sins each refer not so much to a specific act as to a kind of temptation we face: sloth, rage, envy, gluttony, pride, lust, and greed.

Leaving aside love as the cornerstone and self-control as the capstone, we are left with the fruits of joy, peace, patience, kindness, goodness, faithfulness, and gentleness. I think each of these fruits can be lined up one-on-one as a weapon against a specific deadly sin. Here is what my theory looks like.

Joy vs. Sloth

Joy is a state of delight, contentment, and awe as a result of our confidence in the promises of God. Hope is the key to its growth within us. In contrast, sloth is a constant heaviness that says nothing is worth the energy it requires. Sloth is a kind of despair that claims no joy is truly possible, so why bother? Sloth says, "Take comfort at least in resting through this moment, and however many moments you have left."

Joy insists, "Life is about so much more than the comfort of the moment. You were made for worthy participation in grace!" When rest comes, it is not a giving up but only a break before still greater participation in the abundance of life still to come. When we are tempted to give up, to surrender, and to fail to meet our potential, let us hold fast to the fruit of joy growing within us.

Peace vs. Rage

Peace is a state of inner calm and of confidence in the love of God. It comes from surrendering to his will and trusting in his goodness to provide for all our needs. Rage, sometimes also referred to as hate, reflects a desperate effort to take control of the circumstances that frustrate us. Rage claims, "We are our own God, and if we trample on enough opposition or inflict enough hurt on others, it will satisfy the woundedness we feel inside."

Peace knows better. It says, "Screaming, shouting, and especially inflicting our pain on others only add fuel to the fire of our brokenness." Peace tells us to let go of our pain and our fear. "It is only in surrender that we can finally find the assurance and satisfaction for which we so desperately long." When we are tempted to rage, let us pray for a fresh outpouring of the fruit of peace in our lives.

Patience vs. Envy

Patience is an acceptance of both the blessings and challenges of our current state in life. Patience embraces the current moment for what it is and anticipates that more of the story is yet to be written. Envy, on the other hand, anguishes over what it lacks. The envious person sees those who have more and longs to take from them. Envy wants to ascend to the level of the one it envies or, if that is not possible, to at least bring the other down to its level of dissatisfaction.

Patient people know better. If there are burdens to be endured, they do so gracefully, not blaming others. They are grateful for their blessings and also have the self-mastery to face adversity with dignity.

Kindness vs. Gluttony

Kindness actively and enthusiastically pours out blessings on others. Gluttony, on the other hand, is always hungry and never satisfied. The gluttonous person gorges on food and experience. When faced with the opportunity to be generous, the glutton holds back for fear that such an act might, in turn, cost some comfort or pleasure. The glutton is never satisfied. Enough is never enough.

The kind person, instead, has discovered the far greater secret. Kind people, grateful for every chance to give, know in their hearts that giving brings true satisfaction, deeper and longer lasting than any taking could provide.

Goodness vs. Pride

Goodness is a kind of wonder at the beauty of God's design and an embracing of that beauty. Goodness develops as we humble ourselves daily before God, loving his direction and laws. Pride insists, "I will not serve." The proud one dares to claim, "I know better than the Creator what will lead to my satisfaction in life." Prideful people follow God's laws when those laws suit their plans but are content to break them when they don't. Sometimes, proud people do this by dismissing morality altogether. Other times, they rewrite the moral code according to what they consider to be their own superior wisdom.

The good person says, "No one is good but God alone" (Mark 10:18). Good people rejoice at the very opportunity to follow God and are confident that serving him is the very best to which they can aspire. Faced with defeat, the good person accepts the blame and returns wholeheartedly to God, always being renewed in him.

Faithfulness vs. Lust

Faithful men and women honor the covenants we have entered into with others. We are called to be faithful friends, spouses, parents, and children of God. At first glance, some may think that lust only appears to challenge faithfulness in the realm of marriage. If a man gives into the lust of physical desires, he fails to be a faithful husband. I think, however, there is much more to lust than falling into sexual temptation. At its heart, lust says, "Others exist to be used as a means to meet my desires." Tyrants have a lust for power that leads them to trample and control others. In contrast, faithful leaders recognize the dignity of those under them and seek only to serve well. Faithfulness says, "I celebrate the worthiness of each person. I see the reflection of God within every person."

Gentleness vs. Greed

Gentleness is a way of treating others that makes it easier for them to choose the good. Just as kindness and gentleness have a great deal in common, so do gluttony and greed. Whereas gluttony is about consumption and the satisfying of hunger, greed is about hoarding possessions, money, or even ideas. Greed says, "I want more for myself, and I don't care how that affects others."

Gentleness knows not to get caught up in what it does or does not have. Therefore, it is more free to ask, "What do people most need from their interactions with me, and how can I most effectively provide it?" The greedy person cannot afford to be gentle, and the gentle person cannot afford to be greedy.

Well, there you have it—my theory of the interplay between the fruits of the Spirit and the seven deadly sins. You might see a better way of contrasting these aspects of the spiritual life; if so, by all means apply that approach instead. My hope is simply to offer fuel for reflection as we strive to overcome the traps of the enemy and cooperate with God's work of bringing the fruits of the Spirit to life within us.

Acknowledgments

This book never could have come to be without the incredible people God deigned to bring into my life. First, I want to thank my lovely wife, Hollie, who has been supportive in every step of the process, as I snuck away time and again to write just a little longer.

The Word Among Us has been incredible. I feel humbled by the contribution of Beth McNamara, Cynthia Cavnar, and the whole team who helped to create something far better than I ever could have on my own. I want to thank John Wentz, Craig Springer, and everyone at Alpha who responded with such excitement and encouragement about this opportunity. Lastly, I want to thank Tim Glemkowski, who turned to me at a conference in Cincinnati and said he thought I had a book inside me.